The College and the Church

Uneasy Partners

Merrimon Cuninggim

ABINGDON PRESS / Nashville

UNEASY PARTNERS: THE COLLEGE AND THE CHURCH

Copyright © 1994 by Abingdon Press

This book is printed on recycled, acid-free paper.

Scripture quotations are from the New Revised Standard Version Bible, copyright © 1989 by the Division of Christian Education of the National Council of the Churches of Christ in the USA. Used by permission.

Library of Congress Cataloging-in-Publication Data

Cuninggim, Merrimon, 1911–
    Uneasy partners: the college and the Church/Merrimon Cuninggim.
      p. cm.
    Includes bibliographical references and index.
    ISBN 0-687-01151-5 (pbk.: alk. paper)
    1. Church and college—United States—History. 2. Church colleges—United States—History. I. Title II. Title: College and the Church.
    LC383.C86   1994
    377'.8'0973—dc20

                                                 94-36896
                                                   CIP

MANUFACTURED IN THE UNITED STATES OF AMERICA

TO
WHITTY

Contents

Foreword

F. Thomas Trotter, President,
Alaska Pacific University

The world's great religions share a profound sense of wonder about the universe. Contemplation of the world in all its forms and shapes has stimulated reactions of awe, fear, serenity and, especially in Judaism and Christianity, that defining human trait of curiosity.

Awe frames the questions. The questions drive curiosity. Curiosity stimulates reflection. Shared reflection flowers in learning. The psalmist eloquently described the connection between wonder and curiosity in the dramatic Eighth Psalm:

> When I look at your heavens,
> the work of your fingers,
> the moon and the stars that
> you have established;
> what are human beings that you
> are mindful of them,
> mortals that you care for them?
> (Psalm 8:3-4)

The rise of the technological university has obscured for most modern people the profoundly religious origins of schools of learning. The fact is that learning and its institutions are inventions of the religious spirit. The Western university, in particular, is a product of centuries of discourse in Judaism, Islam, and Christianity, culminating in the rise of the first universities in the medieval period.

Christian thought may be understood as the history of reflection on the nature and uses of knowledge. Augustine, Bernard, Anselm, Aquinas, Luther, Calvin, and Wesley each contributed to the tradition of learning as expressive of the religious spirit. When Anselm asserted in his famous dictum, "I believe in order that I may understand," he described the essential unity of faith and learning. It was no accident that divinity was the first faculty in the first universities.

Foreword

To assert the unity of faith and learning is not to assume a history without stress. There has always been a contrary view of intellectual work in the religious communities. So the uneasy relationship between faith and learning persists in our own period. One need look no further than the current struggles in a great American denomination that is painfully separating itself from its magnificent universities and seminaries by a pious positivism worthy of Tertullian's blast: "What has Athens to do with Jerusalem?"

Over the centuries the universities in the West have maintained their independence of church authorities with uneven success but with a steady movement toward autonomy. The questions of control, censorship, and governance have shifted over the years, but the connections have remained visible and, remarkably, honored.

In the New World, the churches perceived learning to be an indispensable element of their self-understanding and mission. Increase Mather liked to use biblical metaphors of wilderness and paradise to describe institutions of learning in the forests of the New World. Learning was seen to be an essential ingredient of the taming of the wilderness and the establishment of a Christian society. Learning was also required for the education of clergy, so essential in the theocratic societies of the first two centuries of European presence in America.

During the eighteenth and nineteenth centuries, hundreds of schools of learning were established by evangelical dominations and the Roman Catholic Church across the landscape of America. The Methodists alone accounted for twelve hundred colleges in that expansive period. Only one in ten survives, but the sheer number expresses the amazing confidence of religious people in institutions and their care for learning.

Somewhere in the last hundred years, the colleges and universities of the churches experienced a perceptible erosion of interest on the part of the church. As is noted in this book, that coincided with the rise of skepticism, the expansion of the land-grant universities, and the overwhelming shift of access after World War II in the public universities.

The churches lost interest in their schools. For some time the churches had ceased understanding their schools in a theologically informed way. What had survived were questions of control and parietal expectations. As pretheological students in large numbers came to be educated in public universities, the last remaining ties to the churches seemed to disappear.

In my own memory, one would expect clergy and laity of a particular denomination to have strong ties with particular colleges. The style and

Uneasy Partners

The College & The Church

Merrimon Cuninggim

Published by Abingdon Press, 1994

From Reviewers

"*Uneasy Partners* is a thought-provoking meditation on the historic connections between churches and colleges. Cuninggim brings a wealth of experience with several church-related institutions, and a clear vision of the values and purposes that are best served by these relationships."

—Nannerl O. Keohane
President, Duke University

"*Uneasy Partners* should be read by all faculty and administrators of church-related colleges (and of other colleges as well)—especially the faculty who are dubious about or, more likely, hostile to their college's church-relatedness. Also, and maybe more importantly, it should be read by church leaders—especially those who wonder why we support colleges which are (in their opinion) at best indifferent to or, worse, an affront to what our church stands for."

—William F. Quillian, Jr.
president emeritus, Randolph-Macon Woman's College

"The list of church-related colleges in the appendix is the most comprehensive one available in print and underscores the great diversity which characterizes institutions which are intentional about their relationship to a particular denomination. . . . No one is better qualified to discuss church-related colleges and universities than Merrimon Cuninggim."

—Harry E. Smith
president emeritus, Austin College

From the Foreword

"Cuninggim clears the table for interested colleges to engage in public discussion about urgent issues of religion and life, the survival of religious institutions, and the role of values in human society. It just possibly might mean an infusion of energy into the churches, which have grown increasingly distracted and irrelevant in recent decades."

—F. Thomas Trotter
President, Alaska Pacific University

About the Author

Merrimon Cuninggim's association with the church and its institutions of higher education has spanned more than fifty years. A graduate of Vanderbilt, Duke, Oxford (where he was a Rhodes Scholar), and Yale, he served as Professor of Religion at Denison and Pomona, and as Dean of Perkins School of Theology at Southern Methodist University. From 1960-1972 he was the executive officer of the Danforth Foundation. After his retirement, he became President of Salem College in Winston-Salem, North Carolina (1976-79) and has served as consultant for colleges, foundations, and educational agencies. His books include *The College Seeks Religion* (1948); *Freedom's Holy Light* (1956); *The Protestant Stake in Higher Education* (1961); *Private Money & Public Service: The Role of the Foundation in American Society* (1972); and *Church-Related Higher Education* (with others, 1979). He has served on the boards of the Association of Governing Boards, the Society for Values in Higher Education, the Council on Foundations, The Foundation Center, and Duke and Vanderbilt Universities.

- -

Name _____

Street Address _____
(no p.o. boxes, please)

City _____State _____Zip _____

Please send me _____copies of *Uneasy Partners: The College & The Church* at the special prepublication price of $8.50 each (plus $3.00 each for shipping and handling) for a total of _____. Publisher's price will be $14.95.

Make check payable to: **Division of Higher Education, BHEM**
Send the completed form and check to:
> Division of Higher Education,
> United Methodist Board of Higher Education and Ministry
> P.O.Box 871
> Nashville, TN 37202-0871

Also, please forward a recommendation to your institution's librarian to purchase *Uneasy Partners: The College & The Church*.

Uneasy Partners: The College & The Church

Merrimon Cuninggim

Chapter Titles

ethos of the churches were defined by their institutions of learning. But ecclesial care diminished as learning and faith were no longer defined in familial or traditional contexts. As care diminished and as demands for wider support increased, the church's schools were required by events to become more independent from their ecclesial parents. Growing complexity in management, governance, support, and constituency increased the disinterest on both sides. Now the majority of colleges that claim some kind of church relationship celebrate mainly historic ties.

As Merrimon Cuninggim has discussed in an earlier essay, the ambiguous relationship between church and college created difficulties of definition. The increasingly independent colleges were generally uneasy with the description "Christian," although they demonstrated extraordinary patience with their church parents. The term that came to be used with widespread acceptance was "church-related" college.

Their status vis-à-vis their denominational parents remained mixed and usually ambiguous. Attempts to write "covenants" between colleges and churches have not always been successful. Most colleges are comfortable with a description of an historical relationship. But direct intervention in the campus by church bodies is increasingly rare.

When I was a college student just after World War II, a committee of Presbyterian clergy annually visited my college to interview administrators and students to ascertain the religious climate of the place. The college's church relationships have continued in forms far more vague than even the clerical visits. But much else has changed on the campuses since then.

Parietal rules came to be the frequent basis of church assessment. Chapel attendance, dress codes, curfews, and separate-sex housing arrangements were normative until the explosive sixties when almost all of that sort of responsibility was shifted to the individual student. That left many in the churches bereft of continuing reasons for supporting the colleges.

Such mentality is caricatured in the story about a mythical college that proudly announced in its catalog that it was located "seven miles from any known form of sin." The strongest emotional appeal to a church support group in the recent period has been to provide security for the students.

During the "time of troubles" in the late 1960s, I was chairman of a United Methodist Annual Conference Commission on Higher Education in Southern California. Our funding was declining dramatically because of dismay about the chaotic situations on campuses. But when a university campus minister addressed the conference about his efforts to protect students from physical danger during an attack on the Bank of America branch of Santa Barbara, there was a surge of positive feeling, and support quickly and generously followed. Churches tend to understand crisis intervention, especially when their children are at risk.

It is ironic that while the religious community was confused about its expectations and students were asserting their autonomy from all forms of parietal restriction, the universities were actually expanding student services in counseling and other services. A whole subset of university administrators emerged from this period. And we discover at one major college an amazingly detailed and published agreement on student behavior in dating, proposing intervention into personal matters far beyond what could have been imagined in the earlier period of churchly ethos.

In the 1960s, with growing anxiety that private church-related colleges would not survive in a time of presumed expansion of federal support of higher education, many denominational colleges reassessed their roles as church institutions. The argument was based on the separation clause in the First Amendment to the Constitution. The United Methodist Church, in a fit of distraction, passed a resolution in the 1968 General Conference that urged their colleges to consider separation from all church connections so that they could survive as independent secular institutions. The Supreme Court decision in *Roemer v. Maryland* (1976) made such panic premature and misplaced, but it reflected the low estate of higher education in the denomination. The church could not articulate reasons for care for its historical mission in learning. The churches generally held indifferent ideas about education and were prepared to move to other seemingly more urgent missions.

To deal with this frustrating situation, I established a research and policy planning "Commission on United Methodist Higher Education" in 1973. Its task was to research the historic and current situation in church-related higher education and to propose new directions for United Methodist attention to a splendid but confused sector. The main report, published in 1976, redefined the questions about church and college relationships. The report suggested that the traditional question, "What is a church-related college?" should be rephrased to be "What is a college-related church?"

These two questions have been at the center of Merrimon Cuninggim's reflections throughout his long career in education and religion. No one is better equipped to comment on these issues than Cuninggim.

He has a keen intellect and a lifetime of association with the church and its institutions of learning. He has earned degrees from Vanderbilt, Duke, Oxford, where he was a Rhodes Scholar, and Yale. At Oxford he became the British Intercollegiate Tennis Champion (1936) and was a quarter finalist in the Wimbledon doubles competition. He has been a professor of religion and chaplain in distinguished colleges (Denison and Pomona). He was dean of the Perkins School of Theology at Southern Methodist University from 1951 to 1960, where he led the school into national academic prominence and successfully integrated the university while he was at it. He was president of the Danforth Foundation of St. Louis when it was a leading force in philanthropy for the support of colleges and universities, including religion in higher education. It was after his retirement that he was president for three years of Salem Academy and College in Winston-Salem, North Carolina.

Throughout his long career, he was active on the national scene as a trustee of Duke and Vanderbilt universities, a board member of the Association of Governing Boards, the Council on Foundations, the Foundation Center, and the Scholars Press; and was active as a consultant to many colleges and foundations. He was a leader in the National Council on Religion in Higher Education, now the Society for Values in Higher Education, a significant group of professors and administrators who gathered annually for a "week of work" and reflected on the roles of religion in education. When he came to the Danforth Foundation, Cuninggim brought the Kent Fellows of the National Council under the Danforth aegis as a partner with the impressive Danforth Fellowship program, which sought to recruit professors in all fields for reflection on religious life and thought.

His books reflect his lifelong passion for church-related learning. *The College Seeks Religion* (1947), *The Protestant Stake in Higher Education* (1961), *Private Money and Public Service* (1972), and *Church Related Higher Education* (with others, 1978) reflect this passion. *Freedom's Holy Light* (1956) explored the role of the First Amendment in preserving religious and political freedom in the nation.

Cuninggim was raised in the home of a college president and observed from his youth the various dramas of university and church life. His academic and public careers took him to the principal centers of learning in the last half-century. More than any other commentator, Cuninggim knows the worlds of academia and the ecclesia. He is at home and respected in both.

I know of no other person whose background more adequately provided him with an opportunity to learn about higher education from experience and reflection. I owe him a great debt of gratitude for influencing my own thinking about higher education and the church.

Foreword

The thesis of this book, reflecting as it does a half-century of active involvement in higher education and in the church, is expressed with startling clarity of those of us who have sought to find ways to claim the churches' attention to learning. Cuninggim suggests that the changed realities of the church and college today force us to the conclusion that earlier formations need to be revised. Whereas at one time the church was the senior partner in the association, the new reality is that the college must now understand itself as the senior partner in the ancient church-college relationship.

This has startling consequences for the administrators of historic church-related colleges. Many of us have awkwardly struggled to keep the flag of church relationship flying. We have tended to let the church pose the question and define the decreasing benefits. Cuninggim presents an invitation to reorder the old debates. His suggestion reasserts the autonomy of the college in the teaching of religion. It furthermore clears the table for interested colleges to engage in public discussion about urgent issues of religion and life, the survival of religious institutions, and the role of values in human society. It just possibly might mean an infusion of energy into the churches, which have grown increasingly distracted and irrelevant in recent decades.

Some years ago the late William Clebsch of Austin Theological Seminary suggested that the churches, in encouraging the state to assume responsibility for the church's institutions of social service, were in fact relegating themselves to cultural irrelevance. The churches' abandonment of colleges fits the same hypothesis. Along with the churches' former hospitals, orphanages, and geriatric centers, the former church-related college slides easily into the expectations of public support. The institutional forms of expression for the sick, the widows and orphans, those left over by poverty and age, and students are no longer understood as the gestures of piety. What is left for the churches' care? What gestures of concern for society survive in the life of the church? Prayer remains, but the leverage of institutional access in the larger society is rapidly disappearing with its institutions.

Cuninggim suggests, against the somber description of Clebsch, that the college may be the church's best hope for survival as a vital center for its life and thought. We all recall that the great reformations of the church have started in university environments. This was true of the first universities, the Protestant Reformation, and the ecumenical movement of the early twentieth century. It may not be too strained to suggest that the college, understanding itself as the active senior partner, may just do it again in the twenty-first century. It's worth thinking about, if the church can still think about such strategies.

Among the bravest and most thoughtful leaders in American religion are the hardy band of presidents of church-related colleges and universities. They will find in Cuninggim's discussion of the "uneasy partnership" some hope that the long tradition of faith seeking understanding will find new forms for the next period.

Acknowledgments

The usual demurrer of authors is fully justified here: the many fine people who helped me are not responsible for errors of omission or commission. This is my own little red wagon, and I've pulled it as best I can.

But those who tried most to show me the way ought at least to have their efforts acknowledged. At one time or another I've sought the counsel of over a hundred who have thought about or worked at some aspect of my subject. Out of that number the following, with various forms of assistance, have been especially helpful: Robert L. Byrd, Dennis Campbell, Penny Cuninggim, H. Grady Hardin, Jeanne Knoerle SP, Thomas Macon, Jr., Samuel H. Magill, M. Kathleen McGrory, Lee C. Neff, Seymour A. Smith, David Trickett, Ken Yamada, and Joan Keeton Young. Seven friends who look through seven different prisms at the field have kindly read the manuscript in its entirety and saved me where they could: Whitty Cuninggim, Robert Wood Lynn, William F. Quillian, Harry E. Smith, F. Thomas Trotter, F. Champion Ward, and John Page Williams. Of all those gentle critics, Bob Lynn was the chief: my notes on conversations galore, in person and by phone, fill a large file-box. For editing the manuscript and steering it to publication, I am deeply grateful to Linda Allen, Sharon Hels, and Jack Keller. When I wanted to stop, the Lilly Endowment told me in their most persuasive way that I had to keep going. And doctors, children, and even grandchildren have played their part in enabling me to see the task completed. To all, my unstinting appreciation.

Merrimon Cuninggim
June 10, 1994

Introduction

The love of the church-related college was born in me, I guess. I first saw the light on the campus of such an institution where my father was teaching, long ago. All my life I have somehow felt at home on nearly every such campus.

The uneasiness about the relationship of college to its parent church may also have been born in me, or almost. My father's professorate was at Vanderbilt; I had no sooner got well acquainted with the campus, perambulatorily speaking, than the University and The Methodist Church cut their ties permanently, each doing part of the cutting. Dad's salary was the only one paid by the church, so he and his family knew what it meant for ties to be cut.

I really don't know when it first occurred to me to do a book on *Uneasy Partners*. Not in the late 1930s, when Duke's President William Preston Few called me on the carpet one Monday morning because of some mild comment I'd made before a neighboring church the day before. Not at the Methodists' Emory and Henry in 1941–42, where the partnership ought to have been uneasy but wasn't. Not at the American Baptists' Denison in 1942–44, where the church and the school traded pleasantries and kept up appearances. Not at the Congregationalists' Pomona from 1946 to 1951, when the relationship was dying but the college's appreciation for its heritage was warm.

The first time I considered doing a book on the ins and outs of college-church contacts was, I think, at Southern Methodist University sometime during the 1950s. I was the Dean of its Perkins School of Theology from 1951 to 1960; and in this job my wife, Whitty, and I had a front-row seat for the "discord and harmony" of such a relationship. Sometime, when things quieted down and got dull, we meant to tell the story.

But they never did—and the next assignment, the Danforth Foundation during the sixties and early seventies, gave us a different perspective. In those days Danforth was still quite a large foundation working almost solely in higher education. One of its advantages over other large foundations was that having its home base in St. Louis made it easier to adopt a national and catholic outlook. We tried not to show preference for one or another kind of college, one or another part of the country—and we almost succeeded.

Another advantage was that Danforth was then the only big foundation engaged in both making grants and running programs—fellowships, conferences, awards, and so on—which required its staff to try to know all sorts of institutions and, even rarer, thousands of their personnel. Paying attention to, say, Harvard, Chicago, and Stanford, and no less to the state-supported giants, we also worked closely with scores, even hundreds, of modest church-related colleges that other foundations had neglected, and with the small, the black, the female, the experimental, and the regional. I would not have learned as much about such institutions anywhere else.

Since my Danforth days I've tried to keep my hand in with both the foundation and the collegiate camps. For the latter, I've continued to work with colleges in a wide variety of activities and through academic associations of several kinds—Association of Governing Boards (AGB), Fund for the Improvement of Post-Secondary Education (FIPSE), the National Endowment for the Humanities (NEH), the Society for Values in Higher Education (SVHE), several church groups, etc.—and when I couldn't run around much more, the urge to put my thoughts on paper finally took hold.

But surely no one in his right mind would ever set out to be an expert on church-related higher education in toto. Any such intention here, let alone any such supposed achievement, is quickly renounced. To take a wide-ranging view calls for both timidity and temerity. I haven't seen enough, but I have seen more than most. As for full-time jobs, I've had six and a half at such schools—the half being Pomona, which in those days couldn't decide whether it was or wasn't church-related. Because of the accident of positions held and people known, I have visited (for whatever that's worth) the campuses of around three hundred church-related colleges, over a third of the total number.

The only bit of arithmetical trivia that may be relevant to the subject of this book is that I happen to have had some intimate contact, involving more than casual work on my part, with over eighty church-related institutions, representing (if that is the correct word) at least fifteen denominations. While counting these strange sheep one sleepless night, it was this last figure that woke me up. It means that I've been so lucky as to have worked with the colleges of some of the smaller denominations as well as with those of the religious big boys. The variety of my tasks has helped me to understand the institutions in their remarkable diversity: teaching, administration, consulting, talent searching, accrediting, lecturing, even trying to resolve disputes. All of it isn't sufficient, but I hope I said it before you did.

And another thing I must say by way of introduction is to note the limitations in this book that even I am aware of. The Jewish colleges are listed but not discussed at all. My knowledge of the institutions of some denominations is much sketchier than of others. My impatience with some churches' propaganda "colleges" is too evident, I fear.

The reader should be alert, most of all, to the fact that this book is not about the colleges per se, even less so about the churches; it strives to hone in on the particular subject of the relationships between the two. Still unwritten, but needed, is a reliable history of that considerable part of higher education that was started by, and continues to be related to, religious groups.

Chapter One

Three Stages of Relationship

Colleges related to a church, any church, are by that fact likely to be among the most misunderstood and often maligned institutions in our society. A third unhappy probability is that they will be admired for the wrong reasons. Misunderstood, maligned, and mistakenly admired are not the same things, of course, though at least two of them could, and nearly always do, exist together.

These unfortunate knee-jerk reactions toward church-related colleges can be found not merely in the untutored public but also among church leaders and academics who ought to know better. But in spite of this, the colleges themselves may currently be as sturdy in their own right as they have ever been. That is, they may be as academically sound and as fully possessed of their own autonomy as they need to be. Not incidentally, they may be as healthy in their relationship with the church as anyone without a peculiar axe to grind could expect.

How can these two seemingly contradictory positions—to be misunderstood, maligned, and mistakenly admired on the one hand, and to be sturdy, sound, autonomous, and healthy on the other—exist together? It is my thesis that such conditions do exist side by side, and probably always will to some extent. But surely the negative opinions about college-church relationships ought to be corrected as far as possible, and the affirmative ones should be expressed less tentatively than they are now. This will clear the way to discuss on its merits the future of the church-connected college and its optimal relationships.

Not So Different in the Early Days

As we embark on that effort, one general observation must be made: the public does not perceive a sharp difference between church-related colleges and all other kinds of educational institutions. It will come as no surprise that, in the ways they are usually conceived, church-related colleges have much in common with denominationally oriented universities, and with seminaries, either as parts of those universities or free-standing.

But it is not often observed that colleges possessing some other kind of outside sponsorship both suffer and enjoy similar swings of circumstance and opinion. State universities are an unexpected case in point: they too are often misunderstood, maligned, and mistakenly admired, all the while making progress as best they can. This is true also for institutions of no formal sponsorship, the so-called independents who have their own con-stituencies: same song, third verse. The details will differ from college to college, sponsor to sponsor, but the underlying problems are akin.

Misunderstanding that is innocent and non-pejorative is perhaps the easiest of all attitudes to deal with. Directed at church-related colleges, it is of a piece with the public's rather widespread puzzlement about higher education in general. When it comes time, a word will be said about the nature and meaning of a college education. Now it need only be noted how confused we citizens are in regard to the subsidiary question, What is an X brand or Y type of institution? Before we get around to criticism or praise, let us acknowledge that we do not always have a useful handle on what a particular kind of college is, what its special status or sponsorship amounts to.

If you doubt it, perform this little experiment on some friend: ask what sorts of institutions are Rutgers and the University of Pennsylvania. Your educated friend will know that both are large, reputable universities; but if he doesn't live in the Delaware River Valley, he may be surprised to learn that Rutgers is a tax-supported institution of the state of New Jersey, whereas Pennsylvania, not to be confused with Penn State, is firmly independent of state control. It might be even more surprising to know that each was at one time a church-related institution. From the sound of the title you can't always tell.

Examples of this confusion are many. For instance, St. Mary's of Mary-land is not Catholic-related, or even ex-Catholic; it is, of all things, tax-sup-ported, a part of the state system of higher education. The University of the South, better known as Sewanee, never did belong to the Confederacy; it has always been related to the Episcopal Church. Auburn, said to be Methodist from 1856 to 1872 and sounding like a private college, formally discarded its less familiar state-supported name, Alabama Polytechnic Institute—it doesn't cheer very well—and thus continues to sound un-state-sponsored. And Purdue is no more distant from the state's tax coffers than Indiana University.

That Rutgers and Pennsylvania once had a church tie is simply an illustration of the state-church relations of colonial days, when every pre-Revolutionary institution was to some degree the cooperative endeavor of both parts of the civic-religious establishment. But church-state divorces, or just amicable separations, took place soon or late in the governance of higher education throughout the new nation.

Some of the early institutions became identifiably dependent on the state—William and Mary, University of North Carolina at Chapel Hill, Georgia, as well as Rutgers. Some gravitated to the church—Yale, Brown, and Princeton for a while, Transylvania to the present. Some fairly quickly became independent of any significant tie in either camp—Harvard, Columbia, Dartmouth, as well as Pennsylvania.

The nineteenth century, especially the latter half, was the heyday of the founding frenzy. Colleges seemed to be spawned in every county-seat town or even in the countryside. It would have been difficult for an outsider to tell one institution from another, one sponsor from another. At this distance, the situation looks chaotic, and it probably was.

Along with the openness of the inviting frontier in fostering this explosive growth in numbers of institutions were two crucial legal-political actions. First was the celebrated Dartmouth College decision of 1819 that, strangely, promoted the establishment of all types of schools, both state and private. A covetous state, the court held, could not take over an existing college. If it wanted an institution of its own, it had to set it up from scratch. And private bodies, that is, churches, were now free of the threat of hostile takeover and could proceed in confidence to establish their own.

The second enabling factor was the Morrill Land Grant Act of 1862, which gave Federal support to the states' efforts. Both the states and the churches were energized thereby, and all in all a horde of mostly weak institutions were founded, largely by churches, and then began to die off in record numbers. Historians estimate that only one in four or five survived. The colleges themselves—that is, the survivors—took on the coloration of their parents, which gave both critic and cheerleader something with which to describe them. It was then that most of today's myths about church-related higher education got started.[1]

With the closing of the frontier in the latter days of the nineteenth century, efforts turned toward giving definition and, as far as possible, substance to the often inchoate enterprise of higher education. Self-appointed "good" colleges of all types banded together to establish the various regional agencies of accreditation, most of which continue to perform their useful judgmental functions today. Lines were drawn between high school and college, and between colleges that measured up and those thought to be of little merit.

In fact, from the Civil War to the century's turn, all kinds of new ideas and new agencies caught the attention of higher education's leaders. Consider the cornucopia: President Eliot began his campaign for the "elective system," as it came to be called, in his 1869 inaugural address at Harvard. President Harper of Chicago conceived the idea of the "junior" or community college in 1900. In between, sharp departures from the usual norm were successfully launched: Johns Hopkins, Clark, Cornell, Stanford, Chicago; women's colleges such as the Seven Sisters; new kinds of graduate and professional education; new subjects, subject-matter societies, and scholarly journals.

The ferment of the time can be illustrated by the questions of crucial academic debate: What about Darwin? Must a teacher have a Ph.D.? Is the model Germany or Oxford? Does football help or hinder? Who should be admitted? Which institutions are the tops? Those last two queries were neatly tackled by two new agencies, the College Entrance Examination Board and the Association of American Universities, both founded in 1900. Early philanthropic organizations, notably Carnegie and Rockefeller, earned both praise and blame from the campuses for their efforts to identify the worthy and support them. The turn of the century, then, and the twentieth's first decade were heady years for taking shape and passing muster for all types of institutions.[2]

We in higher education who are destined to close up the twentieth century would have felt remarkably at home in its early years. The high excitement and large confusion in and around the campus would differ strikingly in the numbers involved, to be sure, for the growth in buildings, money, faculty, students, and just about everything else has been monumental. We have different technology too; we use improved gadgets; we spend time parking and policing. But our joys are the ones they had, and most of the problems we face they too encountered. Earlier it would have been harder for us to identify with the collegiate scene, but from about 1895 or 1900 on, the outlines of their campus life began to be much the same as ours.

For example, students and their consuming interests were coming in for lots of attention, as Woodrow Wilson's plaint makes plain. In 1909, while still President of Princeton, he wrote, "The sideshows are so numerous, so diverting—so important if you will—that they have swallowed up the circus, and those who perform in the main tent must often whistle for their audience, discouraged and humiliated." No wonder he wanted to go to Washington.[3]

Fraternities, athletics, and extracurricular activities were riding high. Since then, the faculty may not have changed very much, but they have certainly learned to whistle louder. A proliferation of administrative positions has arisen to cope with the population explosion of students and faculty. Young women, blacks, Latinos, Asians, and other worthy additions have transformed the look of Mr. Wilson's University and many another. But for all those changes, cosmetic and more, you and I would probably recognize his campus if we were to visit it, or at least we would our own. Church-related colleges were in nearly every regard part of the total picture, befuddled, yet onward and mostly upward.

Church Colleges Around 1900

Historians have told most of the story well. That is, they have called the roll of the acknowledged front-runners—Ivy, near-Ivy, and beacons here and there around the country. The whole collegiate university was enough of a piece, it seemed, that no great harm was thought to be done if attention were limited to the well-situated, the well-supported, and the photogenic.

But the unintended result was that very few of the colleges that caught the historians' eye were church-related, for several reasons. They were less numerous in New England, and some in those parts that had been founded by churches had already slipped their moorings. In the rest of the country they were often more congregated at the bottom than at the top. Yet because they are the chief interest of this chapter, it is important to try to describe them as a group if only to have to admit that they are well-nigh ungroupable.

Let us, then, retrace our steps to focus on the church-related institutions. First, nobody knows precisely how many there were. The number in 1900 was less, but probably not much less, than a thousand. Nearly all of them, no matter what their denominational affiliation, had at most only a few hundred students, but the state-supported and independent schools were also not large.

Paralleling the one-room schoolhouse, still in wide use, was the one-building college. Most church-relateds were housed pretty much in Old Main; and when the Old Mains burned down, as they had a habit of doing, a considerable number of colleges never recovered. A high proportion of them all, burned or not, were impoverished and kept alive only by generous and sacrificing church folk, neighbors and faculty, Protestant and Catholic alike.

The survivors represented a basic urge on the part of the parent churches to provide a moral and religious undergirding for their future leadership. These were the denominations that wanted an educated ministry, and perhaps an educated laity as well. Other sects were not so sure, and thus were slow in developing educational institutions. In the years leading up to 1900, colleges founded by the committed churches seldom challenged their churches' sovereignty over them, nor did other church creations—seminaries, secondary schools, an occasional medical or other facility. They were all in this rich commitment together.

But otherwise the colleges were poor. They were lacking in more than money; they were often pitifully weak in their academic programs. Yet how do we know for sure? Since the lines of demarcation between secondary education and post-secondary levels were not yet tightly drawn, maybe some of the weak "colleges" were quite acceptable high schools. But that's not what they said they were. Compared to the best in the business in their own day (to say nothing about contemporary academic standards), many of the church-founded colleges seemed not much better than marginal.

Yet most of them wanted to be academically strong and tried to be. And for that, as well as for other more sentimental reasons, church-related colleges were nearly always greatly beloved by their constituencies. In *Lanterns on the Levee,* the lyrical chapter on Sewanee differs from other tributes to other alma maters only in the felicity of William Alexander Percy's writing. Even though, or perhaps because, chapel attendance was everywhere required, the chapel itself was the "symbol of college unity and life." To this day, college hymns and songs, written in large numbers when religious services and marching bands felt the need of appropriate music, bespeak ad infinitum their students' affection. Daniel Webster closed his argument on Dartmouth's behalf in its famous Case with these words: "It is a small college, but there are those who love her."[4]

To take an appreciative look at nomenclature and geography: wherever there were more than a handful of people with a common religious outlook, there was likely to be a college, or the remains of one that had not survived the rugged nineteenth century. A town's possession of such an asset could be heralded by the town's own name—and to this day two villages in North Carolina whose schools have long since disappeared are still calling themselves Rutherford College and Yadkin College.

Labelling was more likely, though, to go in the other direction, from the town to the college. It happened with independents and state schools too, of course, but much more often with the churches' creations because there were so many more of them. The college took the name of the crossroad, the hamlet, the town. Gather a group from almost any part of the country: Davidson, Guilford, High Point, Louisburg, Mars Hill, Salem (some North Carolina ones that *did* survive); or Ashland, Findlay, Hiram, Marietta, Oberlin, Rio Grande, Wilmington, Wooster (to name a few Ohio ones); or LaVerne, Loma Linda, Redlands, Whittier (to show the custom got all the way to California). Occasionally a college would become so devoted to its town's name that it kept the name even after it left the town: Pomona, which moved to Claremont; Wake Forest, now in Winston-Salem.

There was often competition among churches for city titles that might lend distinction. I once overheard two Protestants in serious chatter. Said the first: "These Catholics are pretty slick; they name their schools for big cities and get a lot of free publicity: Boston College, Dallas, Dayton, Detroit, St. Louis, San Francisco, Seattle." The other replied, "What about Boston University, Atlanta, Chicago, Denver, Pittsburgh, Syracuse, Tampa—all started by Protestants." The parting whimper was, "But the Catholics were mostly immigrants"!

And the Protestants were mostly farmers. Fearing the lurid sins of the city, they tried to keep their young people away from temptation—which also explains the same location for many of the tax-supported institutions. But the state schools, though equally desiring moral influences, did not choose the names of religious heroes, as did churches for some of their colleges: Calvin, George Fox, Knox, Loyola, Luther, Wesley, Xavier, and Brigham Young. (Notre Dame and St. Whoever fit here too, but what about Bob Jones and Oral Roberts?) If that scheme were too erudite, then churchmen might resort to just the brand name: Catholic, Methodist, Moravian, Presbyterian; with sometimes a touch of the compass—Western Baptist, Eastern Mennonite, Southern Methodist.

It would be impolite to suggest that some of the heroes were honored simply for their money, or that some of the bland names were chosen for easy abandonment, if Santa Claus were ever to come. Surely Duke, Pepperdine, Eckerd, and others were greatly blessed; long ago, John Harvard's generosity was recognized in the same way. But the needy have been known to resist. Back in the 'twenties it was rumored that Mr. Ringling tempted little Florida Southern with $10 million, if only you-know-what. The college trustees' reasoning ran thus: the Methodist Episcopal Church, South (for that was its title then) has its Coca-Cola college (Emory) and its tobacco college (Duke). What would it look like if the Church had "Ringling University"? So they turned it down, the circus king got hit by the Depression, and that was that.

What's in a name? Even Rose is now Rose-Hulman. Yet the cognomens of church-related colleges are filled with hints as to their character. Whatever they now suggest at the end of the twentieth century, they testified at the century's beginning to their locale and their society, their parent church and their faith. Few were national in their perspective, none in their composition. Some were circumscribed in their service—to blacks, or women, or an old-world ethnic group not readily assimilable, or even men. In fact, for a time, a small number conducted their affairs in some language other than English.

Though no college achieved within itself the diversity so widely praised today, the totality of colleges was remarkably diverse. They were not so much limbs of one great tree as they were well-spaced trees in a forest. Moreover, most of the agencies that would relate them to each other did not yet exist: the academics' various councils, guilds, and trade associations. At the turn of the century the ecumenical urge had not yet flowered in either higher education or religion. Despite all this, the total company of the church-related colleges was beginning to be aware of itself.

This growing self-awareness and perhaps self-esteem showed up in many areas and ways, but two are particularly important for our inquiry into college-church relationships. The first flash of self-awareness showed itself in the colleges' concern over the curriculum, which tends to be a secular matter. The second issue was the religious "climate" of the college and the extent to which that was influenced by the affiliated church body.

As for the first, church-related colleges with very few exceptions seem to have participated in the general desire for clearer definitions of academic quality and stronger compulsions to live up to it. Many such colleges were among the founders of the early accrediting agencies; many more wanted to be approved by them. Their own courses of study were largely traditional—the nineteenth century's version of the hallowed trivium (grammar, rhetoric, and logic) and quadrivium (arithmetic, geometry, astronomy, and music)—with heavy doses of the classics, history, and literature. In general there was skeptical resistance to new disciplines and not much election.

Since many of the ablest male students were headed for the ministry or the priesthood, curricula were often tailored accordingly. The religious tinge was spread throughout the course of study, and specific departments of religion were few in number. One of the aims in the founding of the Religious Education Association in 1903 and the Association of American Colleges in 1915 was to encourage more formal study of the Bible and religion in undergraduate colleges.[5]

The secular character of this development lies in the basic question being asked and in the identity of the questioner. The question was, What is the best curriculum for a liberal arts college? And the asker was the college itself. To be sure, the church could have, and in some places might have, raised the question, especially for religious subject matter; but normally it didn't. In most places the denomination was still, around 1990, in firm control of the management of its own colleges; but the colleges themselves were often and increasingly allowed the liberty of asking the educational questions and of acting on them, even when those questions had to do with the study of religion.

The firm control exercised by the churches makes a good transition line to the second manifestation of the colleges' emerging self-awareness: the religious dimension of their character. All the colleges wore some form of pietism or moralism on their habitual behavior, as did many of the state institutions. But the state schools had to be, or seem to be, nonsectarian, whereas the church schools were considered free to be bound to their denomination. The denominations differed so much that the bindings themselves were different, from leader to leader, church to church, and region to region. Whether tied tight or not so tight, however, there was no mistaking the fact that the campuses felt in various ways the presence of the parent church.

My parents could have so testified about the colleges they knew even before they had met. In the late 'nineties and the first decade of the twentieth century, my father studied religious education in the first university that offered the subject, and then he taught it in the second. During the same period my mother taught English literature in three women's colleges: one subsequently closed, the second was taken over by the hitherto male state university across the street, and the third is still struggling. All five, representing three denominations and otherwise quite different, were then plainly subject, though in varying degrees, to their churches.

Not all the denominations were alike, of course, in the rigor with which they supervised their colleges. Sometimes the differences grew out of the nature of the schools: universities usually had more freedom than colleges, secondary schools less; seminaries that were part of a university had more freedom, free-standing seminaries less. More often, the differences were those of the denominations themselves—in polity, emphasis on education, economic status, rootage in society, and other defining coloration. But whatever the differences in kind and degree, all the churches felt themselves to be in charge. And in one important regard, they were: a friendly partnership between church and college was loudly proclaimed, but it was everywhere recognized that the church was the senior partner. Denominations usually did not bother to call the tune on all the campus minutiae, but if the minutiae got out of hand, the church stepped in to restore order when it thought necessary.

The metaphor to hold in mind, however, is not that of the gruff though caring father who took switch in hand when needed. Rather, it is of the would-be protective mother, gathering her compliant chicks around her skirts and keeping them from all harm, including what they would do to themselves if let alone. Some chicks would inevitably want to wander now and then. By the turn of the century a few of the church colleges had begun to flee to the liberty and danger of the big, bad world. But at this time the churches were still in command of their collegiate kingdoms and fiefdoms, and most people seemed to like it pretty much the way it was.[6]

Changes in the Partnership

The chronicle of higher education, aided in recent years by the newspaper that took that title, has been profuse throughout the past nine decades or so. By dint of unending rehearsal we know the story pretty well: changes galore in admissions, size, curricula, finances, dormitory life, athletics, relationships to society, honors, pecking orders, and just about everything else.

But we don't know so well the story of the church-related segment of the enterprise. To be sure, a number of efforts have been made along the way, but those that are not deliberately partial seem to wind up unintentionally so. That is, they may follow the overall story too slavishly, without making clear the relatively minor differences that exist between the church, the state, and the independent institutions; or they may, on the contrary, exaggerate those differences by restrictive definitions and willful, even polemic, interpretations.[7] Mindful not to stray to either side, we shall take note of some of these aberrations in succeeding chapters.

But as much as we need a full and scholarly account of the history of church-related higher education in this country, our purpose here is to engage in a much more limited inquiry, namely, to ask about the shifts during the twentieth century in the relations between the colleges and the churches that established them. Partnership (if that is the right word) is not always dead-equal; it may be weighted on one side or the other, and the weighting may change from time to time. In roughly the last hundred years, at least three different balancings can be identified.

The first is the status that we have just noted, at which the colleges and the churches had arrived by the end of the nineteenth century: the church as the senior partner, the college the junior. The period covered by this position runs approximately from the century's turn to the 'thirties; in some instances to the Depression years, in others up to World War II.

The second form of the relationship is roughly even-steven: neither has clearly the upper hand over the other in normal associations. To give this mutual understanding a time reference is tricky, but with exceptions fore and aft it runs from some time in the 'thirties to some time in the 'sixties.

The third is the period of the colleges' being in the primary position, with the churches' having to play the unaccustomed junior role. This is the time frame we are still in, of course, and are likely to stay. As long as college and denominations want to remain in any kind of fruitful contact with each other, the majority of the partnerships will be those in which the college is the senior.

In positionings of this order, involving sizable numbers of *sui generis* agencies, there are bound to be all sorts of gradations, special circumstances, and blurrings of time and function. One must be careful to state the central proposition with enough room to allow for the imprecise situations that frequently arise, and the unpredictable effect of short-term charisma in one place and episodic bullheadedness in another. But when all is added up, the spread of the century shows a steadily growing maturity on the part of the church-related colleges in the often crucial matter of their relationship with their parent churches. The sketch needs to be filled in with explanatory remarks for each of the imprecise, overlapping periods that have been identified.

In the first period, even when ecclesiastical authority was at its height, it did not go unchallenged. During the early decades of the twentieth century, the church-related colleges as well as society in general attempted to put up obstacles against it. The catalog is familiar: the "war" between religion and science, the expansion of knowledge and thus of the curriculum, a decline in the "cultural authority" of the churches, the stepped-up pace of modern life, the recent rise of the "godless" research university, and other demons.

But some of the ills were not as bad as expected or have been pictured as worse than they were. For example, the supposedly harmful influence of the Carnegie Foundation for the Advancement of Teaching was, and still is, cited. This benefaction, set up in 1906, developed a pension fund for professors. But Carnegie ruled that a college "under the control of a religious sect" could not participate. To become eligible for these funds, a few institutions fiddled with their charters or bylaws, and "at least fifteen" reportedly severed their church ties altogether. I once named eight of these and was amused recently to find that four of them are still listed as church-related. Make no mistake: the efforts by Carnegie and others to set standards in the academic world prompted many colleges to question some of the aspects of domination by the churches. But at the time, the actual defection rate was slight.[8]

Or take the concept of "secularization," widely current at the time and variously defined. Whatever else it means, it usually refers to the erosion of religion and its influence in the collegiate scene. Some folks think this began to happen a hundred or so years ago, and if "secularization" is seen as any departure from what the churches wanted their colleges to be, then its roots do go back that far. But a collegiate fact of the first third of our century is that such important activities as the study of religion and the provision of chaplaincies actually increased on the campuses of church-related colleges—and for the matter, at independent and state schools too. Unless we define words to fit our fancy, we must raise up another villain.

From the denominations' point of view, an alternative villain is not hard to find. It lay in the colleges' beginning to make their own decisions. It was usually they, not the churches, who decided to join the pension movement, expand the religious program, or otherwise manage their affairs. Viewed in the large, however, the friction was minor, and the overwhelming body of church colleges continued through the first third of the century to be subservient or at least respectful.[9]

As for the second period, that of basic equilibrium in the relationship, much of the balance appeared to be the result of mutual withdrawal. Society's upheavals in the 'thirties and early 'forties prompted or strengthened the tendency of church-related colleges to give expression to their own positions. The church was not able to help much in the Depression; the college found it had to make its own way. The church often resisted any new-fangled student behavior; the college usually let them dance. No matter the church's attitude, it was the college that actually signed on for a military unit during World War II—which saved many a campus from going under. When the excitement died down in the late 'forties and 'fifties, the college seldom crawled back under the church's protective custody. How're you gonna keep 'em down on the farm after they've seen Paree?

The instance of church-college discord, as we shall examine in some detail in chapter 5, were nearly all localized, and the publicized separations were as rare as in the earlier period. Some colleges were quiescent, some moribund, and a few died. But others perked up, and a considerable number made the Approved List of the Association of American Universities—now no longer published, but fifty years ago an accepted sign of quality. If a college were on the Approved List, its graduates would readily gain entrance to the best graduate schools. A few blue-ribbon institutions that had not been accepted earlier were admitted on their merits into Phi Beta Kappa, never an easy climb.

New church colleges were still being established in numbers that almost equaled those that closed up or cut all ties with their churches. The Pattillo-Mackenzie study of 1965 estimated that "Eight Hundred Colleges Face the Future." Most of them identified with each other across denominational lines as readily as they did with their own churches' progeny. Here and there a college would pay no heed to the word of guidance from on high, or in the other extreme, would knuckle under to the ecclesiastical authority. But by and large the colleges had come to a status of rough equality with their sponsors, and in the mid-years of the century the partnership was being conducted, usually amicably, on a fairly level field.[10]

As unlikely as it may seem, the influences that made for the third and contemporary state of the relationship between the colleges and their churches have come at least as much from the ecclesiastical as from the collegiate side. To people knowledgeable about higher education, this may appear to be an unwarranted generalization. After all, the highly visible university campuses of the last three decades have become hotbeds of almost everything that can make a campus bed hot—Vietnam protest, drug use, easy sex, athletic scandal, faculty rancor, flawed research, outside interference, and much more. But that is just the point: the colleges' hands were full. Church colleges, by virtue of their often being smaller or less visible, may have had fewer traumas than other institutions, but they had plenty to deal with.[11]

These annoyances by themselves would not make a college want to dilute its cherished institutional ties with its church. On the contrary, they would more likely prompt the college to reach out to the church as a presumably friendly agency that could provide some understanding and support. Left to its own devices, the college would probably not have opted for any major change.

But in the last three decades or so, the churches severally and together suffered problems of their own, of sufficient seriousness as to provoke, or suffer, a further shift in their partnership with the colleges. To be credible, any such judgment needs an exposition, if not in voluminous detail, at least by categories of churches and of problems. I cannot provide a church-by-church accounting, but I want to describe briefly three groupings of the churches whose relationships to their colleges have changed in recent times and are still changing.

The first is the Roman Catholic Church, with the largest group of colleges of any denomination, well over two hundred (see Appendix B). Shifts in status have taken place in the non-Catholic schools for upwards of a hundred years, but they have occurred in the Catholic company in approximately thirty years, reflecting the breath of fresh air blowing throughout the Church from Vatican II and other modernizing influences. Applying the three-stage figure being used in this chapter, one may hazard the view that nearly all the Catholic institutions were junior partners of their Church as late as the 'sixties, but that many have moved rapidly through shared autonomy to the position of making most of their own decisions, in the same manner as their mainline Protestant counterparts. In the title of his Carnegie Commission volume, Andrew Greeley hailed this change as a movement *From Backwater to Mainstream.*[12]

In any group of colleges, the backwaters and mainstreams are hard to identify without being pejorative or inescapably argumentative. But the trends of thought and action in a major denomination's relationship with its colleges are usually identifiable even by outsiders. The Association of Catholic Colleges and Universities has led the way in urging a wide discussion in their membership of such issues as lay governance, academic freedom, and the maintenance of "Catholic identity." Paul Reinert at St. Louis and Theodore Hesburgh at Notre Dame were among the early proponents of lay responsibility in Catholic higher education. A host of other Catholic educators—Alice Gallin, Ann Ida Gannon, Timothy Healy, John F. Murphy, John Courtney Murray, to name only a few—have joined the general discussion, resulting in a growing confidence in Catholic higher education and the heightened status of many Catholic colleges.[13]

The second category consists in the so-called mainline or mainstream Protestant churches, whose colleges constitute by far the largest company in the total count. Most listings of the mainline churches—Methodist, Presbyterian, Lutheran, United Church of Christ, Disciples, American Baptist, and Episcopal (in order of the number of their colleges)—fail to note that roughly a third of the Southern Baptists also belong in this grouping. Moreover, if the "mainline" modifier is taken to mean something about the status of their colleges and the point of view toward education, rather than just size, then relatively small churches, such as Friends, Brethren, Reformed, Moravian, and perhaps others, belong properly in this difficult-to-define category.[14]

There has been little difficulty in recognizing and documenting the long, slow decline of mainline churches in numbers, influence, and spirit. Scholars placed the downward trend at various times and conditions, but it is only in the last thirty years or so, beginning in the mid-sixties, that hands have begun to wring.[15]

What has not been so widely observed, however, is the growing strength of the colleges related to these mainline churches during the time of the churches' decline. Most if not all of the colleges associated with mainline denominations, including most Southern Baptist ones and those related to the small mainline churches, have gained in quality and stature in these recent days. The same is true, I believe, for most traditionally black colleges related to either historically black or white churches. It should not be surprising, therefore, that when colleges are going up and churches down, the nature of their relationship should shift toward a more senior status for the college.[16]

The third grouping of churches is less easily describable, for they aren't all "evangelical" or "conservative"—and these words also apply to some of the churches referred to above. Even "fundamentalist" is not fully applicable, for some claim not to be so. The non-mainline Protestant churches (just for identification) are usually devoted to a strict orthodoxy, though by no means the same one; and if they have colleges, these institutions usually follow suit. This view, please, is not a personal judgment; it is a condition that they, and their colleges when they go along, place on themselves. Many of these churches have burgeoned while ones in the mainstream declined.[17]

Such churches participated little in the massive founding of colleges during the nineteenth century. Most of their educational institutions, more lately established, have stayed close to mother-church, though a few seeking recognition in the academic world have also sought to be less dependent. The "ultraconservative" Christian College Coalition, whose names are noted in Appendix B, are firm in the faith, even if for some it means being nondenominational. Quite a lot of the self-described Bible colleges, while militant in belief, are also nondenominational as well as largely unaccredited. This grouping of colleges is the exception that proves the rule: the less rigid the church, the more open and independent the college. And as even the non-mainline churches slowly evolve, so their colleges can be expected to mature.[18]

To sum up, the present situation as I see it is this: the overwhelming majority of the church-related colleges are still in genuine touch with their longtime founding churches, but for the last twenty-five years or so they have come to be the primary entity of academic decision-making for themselves, with the churches thereby relegated to playing, often unhappily, only a secondary role. For example, it is the colleges who choose their presidents, and in nearly all communions they are usually non-clergy. The only thing strange about that is that some folks still think it is strange.

Exceptions there are, of course. At one extreme are the small group who refuse to let the church be even a junior partner; these colleges have cut the cord completely, for reasons that seemed justifiable to them. At the other extreme are another small group, though slightly larger than the first, who let the churches call their tune to an extent that puts them outside the collegiate mainstream, perhaps geographically but more often philosophically. The first group say, correctly, that they are no longer church-related; the second group say, incorrectly, that they alone are church-related or, scorning mere relationship, that they alone are "Christian."

But the great majority of those who, for the past century and more, have stated gladly their church connection, are possessed of their own working autonomy as educational institutions and rejoice in that fact. The nature and degree of contact with the denominations differ, but the colleges make up their own minds. This is the good news about most church-related colleges today.

Three groups can be expected to disagree with the position being enunciated here. These are, first, some old-line church leaders who draw the collegiate blueprints to their own definitions or desires; second, some secularists who pretty much accept the churchmen's analysis and thus write the colleges off; and third, some recent neoconservatives who are bemused by the past and seek a church-specified resolution. In the next three chapters we shall examine each of these contrary positions in turn.

Chapter Two

Admiring and Demanding Church Leaders

Parents lead the way for their offspring until children can first catch up, and later carry on alone. It is surely a good thing that life is like that, for infants would never make it by their lonesome.

At the beginning, when ecclesiastical bodies first created their colleges, they undertook to perform certain parental duties, assume certain parental perquisites, and lay down parental plumb lines for their academic children. This was more than beneficial, it was necessary; the fledglings had a hard enough time surviving, even with the care and feeding they customarily received.

Back in colonial times, throughout the nineteenth century, and well along into the twentieth, the institutions that churches established (or in rare instances adopted) took on the customs and habits of their sponsors. It would have been surprising only if they hadn't. In nearly every collegiate establishment, ecclesiastics did at least double duty: they tended to their church chores and taught, managed, raised money, and led worship for their colleges. Some did it well and some did it poorly. The church and the college acted and looked alike. No matter; that was the way the college had to start out, and it didn't consider anything else.

But as time passed, the customs and habits began to solidify and be codified into marks and requirements. This development took place in nearly every denomination that had colleges and nearly every institution that acknowledged a church tie. Not all at the same time, of course. Variables were of many sorts: ecclesiastical, geographical, political both of church and of state, ethnic, cultural. But soon or late, the way by which a church-related college could *often* be described came to be the way by which some church leaders (and, though fewer, some academics) thought it ought *always* be described.

For example: The first president was often a clergyman, and before long every president had to be a clergyman. The trustees were usually members of the sponsoring church, and that led to the insistence that they, or some safe proportion of them, always be; and that a good many of them be clergymen as well. And what about the faculty? At the founding they were of course approved, and they ought to continue to be equally approvable, even if by some new standard. Ownership? Strict rules for on-, even off-campus, behavior? Church attendance? Creedal conformity? Yes, all these things and more. The customs became identifying, then defining, marks; the habits became firm requirements.

But while all this was taking place, the two groups of people who helped to produce or establish the recognizable marks of church-relatedness— roughly, churchmen on the one hand and academicians on the other—were beginning to go in opposite directions. Church folks tended to cherish the strictness of a defined relationship, academics to be restive with it. This should not be wondered at. Both groups had their immediate loyalties, and much of the time they did not differ. But when they did differ, each was true to its understanding of what would best serve the institution to which it was primarily loyal—church people to the church, academicians to the college.

Thus it happened that many church-college folks began to desire a looser tie at the time when other church folks without as strong a college orienta- tion wanted it to be tighter. The pattern was imprecise, of course, in nearly every aspect of the relationship. One church might insist, say, on ownership; some other denomination didn't care about that, but thought it wise that the president be a clergyman, or at least a layman in good standing. One college might feel it necessary to provide worship at least twice on Sunday and prayer meeting on Wednesday night; another college simply relied on the local church to minister to the collegiate community.

Churches and colleges, therefore, were of many opinions as to what was desirable in, or even required by, the tie between them. Anomalies, contra- dictions, and above all compromises, were rife. An impartial observer could be pretty sure only that the language used to describe the relationship would please the church, whereas the behavior that embodied the relationship would satisfy the campus. It would be a mistake to suggest that preachment and practice were at cross-purposes, but it would be equally untrue to hold that the college scene always reflected what the church felt was required.

This then was the case in the early years of the twentieth century. Pulling against the leash was at a minimum—there was none at all in the Catholic Church and in other churches of strong discipline, and very little in most of the rest; it was spotty among colleges that strove for academic recognition, and, again, nonexistent among churches that didn't believe in leashes.[1]

But as the century advanced, the colleges matured and began to do their own defining. In both collegiate and ecclesiastical circles the question arose, What does a relationship between school and church mean? What should a church-related college be and do? When academic people posed the question, they gave the kind of answers that the campus itself both prompted and understood (which will be discussed in chapter 6).

But when churchmen raised the question, it was natural that their answers be rooted in the thought processes of a religious community, whose self-understanding might be expressed in creeds or confessions. The churches therefore insisted upon specific requirements for the colleges, and did so precisely during the time when the colleges were getting away from them. In describing this phenomenon, however, exact dating and labelling for whole denominations don't work.

For example, take some of the Trinities in, say, 1910: Trinity (CT), Trinity (DC), Trinity (NC), and Trinity (TX), creations of four different churches, were not like each other, not like all other schools of their own denominations—Episcopal, Catholic, Methodist, and Presbyterian, respectively—but somewhat like their neighboring colleges down the road. Now switch to, say, 1990: all four still exist as just indicated, though Trinity (NC) is now called Duke. But for many churchmen, at least two of the four are sometimes said to be no longer related to a denomination: they don't seem to fulfill all the assumed requirements or have all the marks. Actually, only one, the (CT) Trinity, is no longer counted in its church's list.

Or note the plethora of Wesleyans, named for the founder of Methodism, and the wide spectrum of attitudes they elicit from churchmen: just plain Wesleyans in Connecticut and Georgia, and a few of the state-named ones as in Illinois, Iowa, Kansas, Kentucky, Nebraska, Ohio, Texas, West Virginia, and half a dozen more. Those existing in 1910—and the just-named ones did—had already begun to go their separate ways, as far as fulfilling some Methodist expectations was concerned. Wesleyan of Connecticut finally and amicably broke away; but the rest, in 1990, were connected, a little or more often a lot, with now the United Methodist Church. Yet those people who apply strict signs or marks of belonging might say that none of these measures up, at least not as fully as do the rigorous self-styled Christian College Coalition with "over 80" members, including four non-UMC Wesleyans.[2]

The Alleged Qualifications

It is time to be as systematic as possible about the list of requirements for church-relatedness as viewed by admiring and demanding church folks. When the colleges met these requirements, they were hailed, especially on ceremonial occasions; when the colleges seemed unable or unwilling to meet these requirements, church leaders were unhappy.

The chief marks, followed by my editorial comments in parentheses, fall into the following groups:

1. *Founding and historic association:* The church gave the college birth and has kept in constant touch with it through the years. (Not quite; there were a few raids, defections, and even a conversion or two. But this mark was almost universal.)

2. *Structure and governance:* The church is expected to own and control the college. Methods of control differed, of course, but the church, through some specified ecclesiastical body, was and is the final authority. (It depends upon what you mean by "control"; even "own" isn't always clear. If the body is some other group than the college's board of trustees, then "final authority" needs clarification. Furthermore, the degrees of power and its use differ from church to church, from time to time, from region to region, and from fact to fancy. Treasured as a myth of church-relatedness, this is an unreliable mark.)

3. *Support:* The church supports the college, giving it the sustenance it needs. Not all the support is financial, but that is an important part. (Now wait a minute. Is this ought-to-be or factual? The college would gladly agree that church support is highly desirable, but seldom if ever has it been sufficient—unless one credits the moral kind.)

4. *The credentials of the college leaders:* The church expects the college president to be X, or the trustees to be Y, or two-thirds Y or half Y, or the faculty to be communicants, or seekers, or at least "good" people. The church has a say in the choice of the president, elects all, or the majority, or some, of the trustees, and wants due care to be exercised in appointing the faculty. (Trying to state this requirement in general terms ends in making it look both impossible and absurd. But in its local specificity this mark is serious, onerous, and mischievous.)

5. *The students:* Some churches once expected, and maybe wanted, all of their own kind, or at least most—unless they meant to proselytize, which was rare. Now the student body nearly everywhere is polyglot, and a church

might simply hope to get enough of its own for them to feel at home on the campus. Who is counting? (I was once President of a small church's small college that had more Moravians on the board than were in the faculty and the student body combined; but the Moravian Church thought of Salem as church-related, and so did Salem.)

6. *The course of study:* Almost without exception, the churches that spawned colleges wanted not an indoctrinated but an educated ministry. In simpler times this usually meant studies in religion, or more broadly, the liberal arts and sciences, or the Western and Judeo-Christian traditions. But such a general curriculum was not peculiar to the church-related colleges; all of them, of whatever sponsorship, offered much the same thing. Differentiation, then, was to take place by way of requirements: the church colleges mandated more Bible study or theology or doctrine. (Trouble was, this insistence never quite took shape. Sometimes would-be clergymen would go to unapproved schools, or Bible study was left to the home and Sunday schools, or the curricula of non-church-relateds were too much like those of the relateds. Lots of pious people felt this mark ought to be distinctive, and often pretended that it was, but the argument was seldom convincing.)

7. *Campus life:* As with other categories, this mark of church-relatedness has two versions: an ought-to-be and an it-is-so. Most colleges gave up the it-is-so claim long ago, for students could always be counted on to sample the available sins; but many schools felt their church tie required that they hold high what ought to be. Proscriptions against cheating, dancing, drinking, drugs, and promiscuous sex were everywhere. (Lasted longer too, and you can still find some church colleges that have sharply restrictive standards for student behavior. But when the bishop's darling daughter walked out on the dance floor, the rules began to look a little silly. I know, for I took her.)

8. *Religious affairs and provisions:* A church-related college takes the work of the church seriously—worship, study, service, or whatever the denomination insists on. Therefore, the colleges makes adequate provision for the religious life in all its usual manifestations: course, chapel services, exercises of moral conscience, religious commitment. (That this is part of the inescapable obligation of the church-related college will be argued in chapter 6. Now, however, we must note that it is not a definitive or exclusive mark. Many such colleges don't do a very good job in this regard; and many independent and even tax-supported ones outdo them on occasion.)

9. *Ethos:* The church expects the college to be fully what the church itself is, and says it is. This is a matter of proclamation, but more importantly it is a matter of being, of identity. The church defines itself, and thereby defines its college, at least in its aspects of faith, of creedal position, of institutional essence. Thus the college's testament of faith is a reliable mark of its church-relatedness. (A number of caveats spring to mind: Identity is not the same as identicality, and a college is not the same as a church. A college needs to make its own testament of faith, or mission, or purpose; and when it differs from its church's, it may still think of itself as church-related—though some churchmen may not. Moreover, public announcements of faith, or purpose, are often couched in language that substitutes felicity for accuracy. Watch out for ethos, and for who is doing the defining.)

So there we have the qualifications, or identifications, or marks of the church-related college, as widely viewed toward the close of the nineteenth century and in the early years of the twentieth. Let us be mindful, however, that each of the nine noted above is not a single item but a catchall for a considerable number of specificities and, largely by church leaders rather than academics, insistencies.[3]

The Losing Effort to Codify

The colleges reacted in a predictable variety of ways, depending on their age, maturity, overall quality, and breadth of perspective. Some of them, deeply beholden to the church, accepted the expectations placed upon them and fulfilled them as best they could. At the other extreme, a few renounced the relationship entirely, some with a bang (such as Vanderbilt), others more quietly. The majority went along with what wasn't worth arguing about, chafed a bit here and there, ignored what they felt they could, and debated the pros and cons of other items, sometimes winning.

Churchmen understandably wanted a reliable definition to deal with, both for descriptive purposes and, when the colleges didn't agree, for holding them in line, in public claim if not in fact. Historians and other students of higher education wanted the same thing for different reasons: to accept the marks as conceived by others made their task of interpretation easier. As the century proceeded, and as the colleges themselves began to outgrow their former subordinate status with their denomination, church leaders began to insist that the colleges live up to the old marks, give affirmation to the old ties, and adopt the old behavior. That the old marks, old ties, and old behavior were going, going, gone, seemed not to matter; the labelling took place anyway.

It was a case of bad timing. Furthermore, the litmus-test approach and, when possible, the use of a straitjacket seldom worked. Everybody's-out-of-step-but-Johnny soon became everybody's-out-of-step-*with*-Johnny. Times were fluid, of course: Methodist and Presbyterian colleges were usually rumbling before Catholic and Southern Baptist ones, and urban before rural. Yet soon or late during the century's middle years, the supposed marks of church-relatedness were more recognizable in the breach than in the observance.

It happened more by accident than design that, prompted by other interests and duties, I took a look at the church college scene in roughly twenty-year intervals, during 1938–41, 1958–61, and 1978. In the earliest of those pulse-takings, the standard description of the church-related college didn't quite fit. By the middle period, the confusion was such that some institutions reported one status to one query and another status elsewhere. In the third inspection, I concluded that only a broad spectrum rather than a tight encapsulation could give a credible picture of the church college scene. To codify had come to be a losing effort.[4]

But some folks did not want to give up. The first massive examination of the subject was by Manning M. Pattillo and Donald M. Mackenzie, entitled *Church-Sponsored Higher Education in the United States* (1966), preceded by their shorter report, *Eight Hundred Colleges Face the Future* (1965). Taking the universe of church-related colleges within their broad view, they saw all the characteristics and practices mentioned above, and realized that one defining formula would not suffice. They identified three "models": the "defender of the faith college," the "non-affirming college," and the "free Christian (or Jewish) college." But even with a well-greased shoehorn of explanatory language, not all the schools seemed to fit in.[5]

The basic trouble with the Pattillo-Mackenzie typology, I think, is the pejorative nature of the labels they chose to use. "Defender of the faith" is meant to be mostly admired, though the authors concede that "there are relatively few institutions in the United States that fit this description." "Non-affirming" has a negative sound, and the authors describe such a college in largely negative terms. "Free Christian" is meant to be affirmative, and this is the kind they recommend. Such a college "is free because it does not control thought, Christian because it has a definite commitment."

In the authors' minds, it "combines the chief assets of the other two models while it tries to avoid their liabilities." The longer study admits, "Many colleges purport to be this kind of institution, but only a minority actually exemplify it."[6]

The titles of these types of colleges are more likely to have been chosen by church than by collegiate leaders, and more likely to have been resisted by the latter. Since Pattillo and Mackenzie thought only a few could qualify as being exemplars of the first or the third model, their study seemed to encourage the notion that the majority were "non-affirming," a put-down that the colleges themselves would not have agreed with. In other words, Pattillo-Mackenzie fell into the trap of categorizing the colleges on the basis of alleged marks or qualifications that church leaders had once set or hoped for, but that no longer accurately described the institutions.

It was an attractive trap to other scholars as well. The theory seemed to run to this wise: if none of the supposedly defining marks is by itself sufficient, all together they may yet add up to something close to a reliable description. For example, Richard E. Anderson of Teachers College, Columbia, confessing his dependence on the Pattillo-Mackenzie study, developed what he called a "religiosity index" using "eight variables":

> percentage of full-time equivalent students of the same religion, percent of total church support, religious requirements for members of the governing board, required chapel attendance, compulsory religious courses, strict moral demands placed upon students (e.g., no smoking or dancing or required missionary service), statement of religious purpose in catalog, and specification of denominational ties in the catalog.

Anderson explained, "Institutions which scored below three on the index were considered secular."[7] Considered by whom? By Anderson himself, of course, but his study was published in 1977, and the colleges had long since abandoned the gospel of marks. Those who sympathized with the Anderson approach were some of the church leaders who still held their collegiate children's feet to the fire, and a few of the more compliant children. But by this time the large majority of the church-related colleges had quit such self-congratulatory counting.

Lest we dismiss too quickly the practice of setting up rigid definitions and qualifying marks, let us consider what Anderson was really suggesting. Although a college does not need to own to all "eight variables" in order to be "religious," it does have to have at least three; but any three will do, it seems. Yet if it is as few as three, then how reliable are these factors? The hunch is, they are not reliable at all in measuring the degree of church affiliation. Highly unlikely as it might seem to tight-binders, it is still possible that some institution with, say, a score of two would be more genuinely related to its church than some other with a score of six or eight.[8] The numbers game once worked, perhaps, when colleges were malleable, but a backward look is still just that.

One more illustration of this temptation to pin labels and take totals should suffice. Intending to "replicate in part" the Pattillo-Mackenzie study, a junior dean of a quite conservative college developed a questionnaire to get at the present condition of college-church relationships. His summary item ran as follows:

The current status of your institution's affiliation with a religious organization may best be summarized as (check one of the following):

_____ very religiously related
_____ moderately religiously related
_____ slightly religiously related
_____ not at all religiously related

"Religiously related" was not defined except by implication from the preceding questions that had to do with the composition of boards, the amount of financial support, preference in the selection of faculty, and so on. The respondent was invited to add one plus one plus one, and if the total was high enough, then surely, the reasoning ran, the level attained would be "very." But it doesn't work that way. Even the "very" related colleges by this method of calculation might object to the arithmetical way they got there.[9]

Occasionally a church-defining magazine or a graduate student writing a dissertation may still construct a formidable checklist for trying to identify the provably pious among the colleges. Groups of institutions that continue to put large store on marks that qualify and creeds that define are now banding themselves into various associations of the like-minded, and are testing the accreditation process.[10] To the extent to which these efforts seem related to a recent neoconservative thrust in educational philosophy and in church politics, we shall return to this development in chapter 4. But for now I'll note only one further effort by a late twentieth-century thinker to hold on to early twentieth-century patterns of church-college relations.

William C. Ringenberg's book, *The Christian College: A History of Protestant Higher Education in America,* published in 1984 by the Christian University Press, is an admittedly selective treatment. The breadth that seems to be promised in the title is not delivered, for "Christian" is nothing so amorphous as "church-related." The author says there may now be "perhaps 200" colleges of the "Christian" variety, and to get that large a number he has to stretch his own parameters.[11]

Ringenberg relied heavily on his mentor, Mark A. Noll, who wrote the "Introduction" which traces "Christian Worldviews and Christian Colleges" pretty much up to the present. In his last two sections, "The Recent Past" and "The Path Ahead," Noll's emphasis is on "evangelical" colleges, and he seems to dismiss from his concern the host of church-related institutions that do not qualify in his mind as "Christian." His treatment begins as a broad-gauge view and ends as a narrow outlook.[12]

Once Ringenberg's history reaches the twentieth century, he adopts Noll's tactic: nineteenth-century collegiate foundings by churches are painted with a broad brush, but "most of the institutions which remain clearly Christian today are aligned with conservative Protestant denominations" such as the Assemblies of God, the Churches of Christ, and the Free Methodists. The villain that made so many "liberal Protestant" colleges fall outside his definition of "Christian" was, of course, "secularization"; he deals at some length with its "sources" and its "marks," and for most of the twentieth century, he feels, most of the church-related colleges of the mainstream churches do not measure up.[13]

In his section on the "Marks of Secularization," Ringenberg reveals what he thinks a "Christian" college should be. Using "mark" negatively, he finds seven factors that disqualify a college from claiming Christian status: (1) statements by the college that are "equivocal" rather than "explicit"; (2) less emphasis on "Christian" in faculty hiring; (3) teaching the Bible only as a part of general education; (4) decline in chapel and religious activities; (5) a drop-off in church affiliation; (6) unfriendly budgetary decisions; and (7) the loneliness that "Christians" on campus begin to feel.[14] But not all Christian colleges can be disqualified by using Ringenberg's standard.

If his marks of secularization are turned around and phrased positively rather than negatively, they sound like the marks of old that church leaders once tried to demand of their colleges. Ringenberg's "history" of Protestant higher education calls for our attention because it shows the danger in thinking of church-related colleges in sharply enumerated requirements of belief and behavior. When he defines what a "Christian" college must be, he leaves out Catholic institutions entirely and denigrates the Protestant ones that don't fit his formula—which is most of them.[15] We continue to need a full-fledged chronicle of church-related higher education that is all-inclusive, and credits the good faith of both churches and colleges that do not agree with his strict formulas.

People of the churches have nearly always loved their little colleges and in recent days the big ones too. When some leaders began to misunderstand their growing up, and when they sought compliance with churchly rules and interpretations, the colleges' reluctance and even refusals to abide by all such expectations did not mean they were no longer church-related. It meant that the colleges simply did not always fit the churches' prescriptions for them. Colleges and churches still clung, and cling, together.

To be misunderstood, and even maligned, by those who are thought to be close is hard. To have the same sort of thing come at you from the opposite direction is also hard but strangely reassuring. We shall now turn in the following chapter to the attitude of outsiders, who in distinction from churchmen might be called secularists.

Chapter Three
Denigrating and Confused Secularists

The word *secularist* is as elusive and imprecise as *churchman,* maybe more so. The latter term is out of favor these days because of gender sensitivity, but "churchperson" just won't do, and multiple-word descriptions get in the way of linguistic rhythm, if not more important things. No matter; when reference is made herein to the churches' misunderstanding of their own colleges, the individuals involved were nearly always church-*men.*

But since "secularist" is gender free and otherwise largely nonaligned, it may be used more loosely. Even for our limited subject it can cover a wide range of observers and critics, including intellectuals both within and outside the academy. The secularists in this chapter's title are the considerable number of learned and influential commentators, early and late, whose attention to the church-related colleges, or often the lack of it, was governed by a non-church stance. Their perspective was not motivated by concerns about religious faith, regardless of its variety or their personal allegiances, if any. Rather, they simply looked at all colleges, and thus at each particular kind of college, from what they took to be a non-religious, though not necessarily an irreligious, point of view. It was simply as educators that they spoke.

Thus the secularists, like the churchmen, were not a tightly defined group. In fact, from the latter years of the nineteenth century to the present, the two groups have had several other things in common. To try to do justice to both companies, it should be pointed out that there was actually some overlapping. The people who used the insights of religion to examine their colleges might be the same folks who applied educational yardsticks to them. And to make things even more complicated, the churchman-educator or believer-skeptic was not always on the outside looking in; he (and an occasional she) might be a member of the faculty, or even the president. The lines of demarcation were muddled. But before reviewing the perspectives of individual thinkers, an overview of their position is in order.

Differences with Religious Leaders

Strangely, the point at which the churchman and the secularist chiefly agreed served as the beginning for their sharpest delineation.

Consider: secularists brought no special definition of their own to the task of observing the church-related colleges. They accepted the proposition that the term was roughly accurate: the colleges were somehow "related" to their sponsoring denominations. Thus as the church leaders began to compile lists of qualifications, or marks, for identifying these institutions, the secularists usually went along in easy, even thoughtless, acceptance, unless they had some firsthand experience to the contrary. Time passed and some of the colleges challenged the supposed markings, but the secularists continued to uphold the mistaken assumptions they had learned earlier from the churchmen.

Cataloging the colleges under the same outmoded rubrics of definition, however, is different from having a similar attitude toward them. For example, both church folks and secularists might swallow the shaky proposition that denominations were in firm control of their colleges, but the one side would hail and the other deplore such a notion. Ecclesiastics were sometimes charged with being defensive and pretentious, of holding the line and trying to retain at least the trappings of control. The secularists' contrary position was expressed first as a lack of appreciation for, and then a lack of knowledge about, church-related higher education.

Because of their lack of appreciation, the secularists contributed an addendum to the body of identifying marks that the religious people had drawn up and tried to insist on. The areligionists settled on the questionable opinion that the church colleges were nearly always near or at the "tail of the procession," as David Riesman used the term, and further, that this trait of academic mediocrity was the inevitable result of church-relatedness. If any college fulfilled all the items that the church proclaimed and the secular world accepted, then that institution was expected to be, at best, second-rate.[1]

The low estimation of these colleges was followed closely by a high degree of ignorance about them. It was almost as if the secularists had said, "Since the colleges are no good, why should we bother to find out about them?" In any event, many didn't—and in the process they influenced a lot of other outside agencies to ignore the schools that the churches were presumably controlling, regulating, and supporting. The state of ignorance leads directly to active negligence; lack of knowledge breeds lack of notice. Philanthropic foundations, and other organizations that rank colleges, bestow honors, and give out scholarships—these agencies did not pay the same attention to the church-related colleges because, among other reasons, they did not know them as well as they knew, or thought they knew, the independent and the front-line state schools.

The impression must not be left, however, that all ignorance and disrespect were on one side and all knowledge and regard were on the other. Church people could be as ill-informed and dismissive of their own colleges and those of rival denominations as the elitist secularists. And the secularists, whether elitist or homespun, could on occasion both understand and appreciate an individual church-related college. It has been fashionable, for example, to praise most Quaker or Episcopal colleges, or ivy-coated others here and there, as tokens that at least some church-relateds can be excellent. Once again for this discussion, the categories are not set in concrete. But in the main, the secularists outdid the religious observers in being confused about the character of church-related higher education and in denigrating what they thought it amounted to.[2]

The disparagement of church-sponsored colleges may have begun in the latter part of the nineteenth century. Historians tell us that that was the time when the university idea took over, which was true; and that Charles Eliot, Andrew White, Daniel Coit Gilman, and others in the new or rejuvenated research institutions, had little use for religion and thought ill of the church-related colleges, which was not necessarily so. The university idea did not necessitate the rejection of religious faith, the institutions themselves did not bar religious expression from their campuses, and most of their presidents and other leaders went to some church every now and then. What they thought about the church schools was certainly not the same as what the church leaders thought and what the schools believed about themselves. But these two bodies of opinion, or three, all perhaps poorly informed, were not unrelated to each other.[3]

The relationship was mostly in one direction. It was the church that did most of the defining, and the church college went along; that definition was pretty much accepted by the secular university, newly convinced of its own rigorous mission. When the church leaders set up their standards—one, two, three, etc.; see the preceding chapter—it wasn't long before the secularists seemed to believe them more than the church's own colleges did. Being gullible, the secularists started describing the colleges as the churchmen were wont to do, not realizing that many of the colleges themselves had begun to question the marks. The main difference between the secularists' and the churchmen's outlook was in the expected result: the secularists believed that those marks would lead to mediocrity.

But there was always a little independence of judgment, a modicum of give-and-take, between churches and their colleges, and between either or both and the secularists. Around 1900 the new research universities led the way in setting up accreditation agencies, and church colleges often helped out and made the grade. When I first looked at this question in 1940, well over half of the 724 accredited institutions were, by any definition, church-related. The banner research group, the Association of American Universities, founded in 1900, set up an "approved" list of institutions whose graduates were acceptable in the AAU graduate programs; of the 289 schools on that more restrictive list in 1940, roughly a third, depending on definition, were church-related. Phi Beta Kappa, surely the most elite form of "accreditation," found place for over fifty.[4]

Not-all-bad must ever be balanced with not-all-good. The observer of this diverse and complicated segment of higher education dare not state one corrective without its opposite number, for each biased opinion was matched by another. The admiring churchman must be reminded that too few of the church-related colleges have achieved academic distinction, and in the same breath the denigrating secularist must be persuaded that some of them are institutions of quality.

Two Kinds of Disrespect

The title of this section could have been "*Three* Kinds . . . ," for one of the favorite forms of treatment was no treatment at all. Through the first half of the century and even into more recent days, general books on higher education often omitted any discussion of church colleges, or the dash was so slap that full omission might have been fairer.[5]

As we have seen, the two kinds of disrespect that secularists often practiced were: (1) the easy acceptance of the churchmen's list of marks of identity for the church-related colleges at the very time when the colleges themselves were pulling away from the marks, though not often from the church; and (2) the lack of information about the colleges. So closely were these attitudes related that it was almost as if the secularist were saying to himself: "If so-and-so is what the churches think their colleges are or ought to be, why should I question their position?" quickly followed by, "Why should I bother to learn about such colleges?"

The Carnegie Commission on Higher Education, chaired by Clark Kerr and broadly representative of the best scholarship available, meant no disrespect to any part of its whole subject. When it undertook a spectrum of studies in the sixties and early seventies, it commissioned two volumes to cover the church-related colleges, one each for Catholics and Protestants.

The volume treating Roman Catholic colleges was entitled *From Backwater to Mainstream: A Profile of Catholic Higher Education* (1969), written by Andrew Greeley, the well-known priest and scholar, a sociologist by training. By virtue of his already having written voluminously in the field, Greeley emphasized the "immense diversity" of institutions ("from Immaculate Heart to the University of Dallas"), and did not try to establish a typology.[6]

Its somewhat companion volume, *Education and Evangelism: A Profile of Protestant Colleges* (1972), whose author was C. Robert Pace, examined a much larger group of institutions. In order to do this, Pace offered two breakdowns. The first categorization, to which Clark Kerr alludes in the Foreword to the book, identified "four major types":

1. Institutions that had Protestant roots but are no longer Protestant in any legal sense[;]
2. Colleges that remain nominally related to Protestantism but are probably on the verge of disengagement[;]
3. Colleges established by major Protestant denominations and which retain a connection with the church[;]
4. Colleges associated with the evangelical, fundamentalist and interdenominational Christian churches.[7]

Let us note what these first "types" amount to. Type 1: What does "in any legal sense" mean? It sounds as if an institution isn't Protestant unless it is so in some "legal sense." Yet scores of longtime Protestant colleges are not legally or organically connected with a church, but are still church-related in their own eyes and the denomination's. Type 2: What does "nominally" mean? Why "probably"? And who decides "on the verge"? Type 3: "major"? Why don't non-major, presumably smaller, denominations count? In any event, this large grab bag could properly include nearly all the colleges in types one and two. Type 4: Is the first use of "Christian" in the typology meant to suggest that the colleges in the preceding types fall short? Of the three polysyllabic adjectives, the first two are fairly clear, but what are "interdenominational Christian churches," and what are their colleges? Does he mean simply ecumenical? Then they don't fit well with "evangelical, fundamentalist" ones.

The wording of the four types and their order of listing raise more general questions: Is the author implying that colleges of type 1 no longer belong, that type 2 are on the way out, and that type 4 are the preferred group? Is this the view of the colleges themselves? Isn't it likely to be the view of the churches or, more likely, of only "the evangelical, fundamentalist" churches? How did it happen that the book from the prestigious Carnegie Commission dealing with the Protestant colleges accepted some of the outmoded marks of old-line churchmen (and their neoconservative followers; see chapter 4), and thus omitted many of the strongest colleges? Does the author really believe that the future belongs to type 4?

Pace's second categorization answers some of the questions posed by his first, but raises some new ones:

[1] a group . . . originally Protestant . . . now largely if not totally independent. . . . Their present reputation is owing . . . to the character and quality of their educational programs.

[2] the strongly evangelical and fundamentalist colleges.

[3] a third group . . . that have neither a national reputation based on educational programs nor any strong support from the churches . . . tepid environments . . . neither warmly spiritual nor coolly intellectual.

This time it looks as if the author has fully adopted the secularists' addendum to the churchmen's mythical marks: the colleges lost to the churches are those that have achieved academic strength (type [1]). The favored group now seems to be only "the strongly evangelical and fundamentalist" (type [2]). The "third group" must have been established by the church at Laodicea. All in all, Pace's "profile of Protestant colleges" is no such thing, for the great majority of them would not know that their picture had been drawn.[8]

"The Tail of the Procession"?

Even more disappointing is the inadequate treatment of church-related colleges by the distinguished scholar David Riesman, best known perhaps as the author of *The Lonely Crowd.* Throughout a long career he has written widely on the concerns of higher education in general; he has never felt, as some of his secularist colleagues have often done, that he should bypass or ignore the church schools. Rather, he seems simply to have accepted old-line churchmen's ideas as to what such colleges were, with the outsider's addition that the marks they were said to possess made them, with few exceptions, inevitably mediocre. Thus his view of Protestant, and to a lesser degree Catholic, colleges is inadequate and, sorry to say, sometimes factually mistaken.

Riesman's first influential book in the field, *Constraint and Variety in American Education,* was based on lectures given in 1956 and went into several editions. His compact treatment of "The Academic Procession" is wide-ranging, full of facts, and often sharp in its judgments. He deals gently with Catholic institutions, perhaps because he knows them less well. His section, "Torpor in the Tail of the Procession," is reserved for Protestant colleges, which he also seems not to know well but is quick to disparage. Pointing out the "enormous distances both within and among Protestant denominations in terms of the degree and severity of church control," he accepts the churchmen's old aspiration rather than the colleges' new status; at the time of his writing, "degree" was still present, but "severity" was almost gone. In fact, "control" was no longer the accurate word.[9]

The Academic Revolution, of which Riesman was a joint author with Christopher Jencks, came along twelve years later and is encyclopedic. Writing from a secularist and elitist point of view, the authors try to describe the collegiate scene fairly and sensitively, and on many matters of importance they succeed, sometimes brilliantly. In his Preface to the 1958 edition of *Constraint and Variety . . . ,* Riesman notes how hard it is to get reliable information about the colleges; *The Academic Revolution* confirms the large effort the authors made to overcome the difficulty.[10]

But in the two chapters in which they deal with our subject, they leave much to be desired. "Catholics and Their Colleges" covers seventy-one pages, in sharp contrast to the twenty-one given to "Protestant Denominations and Their Colleges," a vaster field by far. The analysis of the Catholic institutions points out that, of the 260-odd, less than two dozen were diocesan; "the rest [were] operated by autonomous teaching orders." "The result has been pluralism verging on anarchy . . . hardly less complex than among Protestant colleges." A lengthy section on "Control" notes great differences among the orders, battles with the hierarchy, and the recent beginning of lay presidencies and lay boards.[11]

As to this latter development the authors seem ambivalent. On the one hand, they accept the church's time-honored form of college management, and express the opinion that "the best Catholic colleges have found better clerical leadership than their Protestant counterparts." (Which makes one want to ask, How do they know? What is "better"?) On the other hand, they admit that "the eventual triumph of lay professionalism is likely if not inevitable." At the end, they wonder whether the church's colleges will "remain 'Catholic' in any recognizable sense"—by which they mean, whether the colleges will measure up to the marks the church has set for them.[12]

The authors' short-changing of the Protestants is less gingerly, less knowledgeable, and less sympathetic. Once, these colleges were almost the whole story, but now they are viewed as "hardly consequential." The Section on "Natural Selection and Evolution among Denominational Colleges" concedes that during this century some of them have been "caught up in the academic revolution," that there have been slow gains for "erudition" versus "piety and orthodoxy," and that "colleges were gradually becoming more self-directed." "The net result . . . was that while most started out as narrowly sectarian establishments very few remained that way." So the academic gains were really losses for the faithful if one accepts, as Jencks and Riesman seem to do, the old-line definition of what church-related was supposed to mean.[13]

They believe that "several hundred have dropped their church ties and have become officially non-sectarian"; and so they hail "the triumph of academic over clerical values." But whatever "dropping" means, the figure is too high; and "church ties," "non-sectarian," and "clerical values" are not defined. Speaking of Swarthmore and Oberlin, they postulate that "the unusual level of concern with social and moral issues may be rooted in the religious past." But "unusual" and "may" and even "the religious past" are loaded. Do they mean to leave the reader with a notion that the good colleges are not tied and the tied are not good? What makes some of them untied? Simple: they don't have the marks.[14]

Those that do have the marks are given special treatment in the section, "The Holdouts Face the Future"—holdouts, that is, not from the church but from "The Academic Revolution." Such a poor, "lower-middle class" college will not improve "unless it reinterprets its denominational commitments in largely secular terms." Colleges that are "sectarian"—that is, church-related; Jencks and Riesman make no differentiation between the two—"cannot compete academically with their non-sectarian rivals."[15]

It is as the summary word of this section that the authors produce the oft-quoted paragraph beginning, "The survival of recognizably Protestant colleges . . . ," with its dire prediction of their future. Their only chance is that "enclaves whose members believe passionately in a way of life radically different from that of the majority" will pay the price "for a brand of higher education that embodies their vision." "Enclaves" are identified as a potpourri of special groups: Mennonites, fundamentalists, Brigham Young, "the radical right," Pepperdine, Wheaton of Illinois, Bob Jones, and more, all of which are indigestibly lumped together, denigrated and dismissed, many being misinterpreted in the process.[16]

But not all of these enclave institutions would claim that they are the only unsmirched Protestant ones left. Certainly the vast majority of church-related colleges would resist the implication that they have bowed to Baal. The trouble lies at the start of the summary paragraph, in the overtones to the word, "recognizably." What do they mean by it? Throughout their chapter on the Protestant colleges, they seem to have adopted without question the view of such schools, part long-ago fact and part dashed hopes, as held by the churchmen of fifty or more years before. Jencks and Riesman are saying that the colleges now must live up to the picture then, or else forfeit their right to be thought related to their church.

Such an unfortunate misunderstanding, consisting of the secularist's succumbing to the churchman's early desire, is based on a lack of knowledge of the church-related colleges both generally and specifically. In 1981, Riesman wrote a paper entitled "The Evangelical Colleges: Untouched by the Academic Revolution." Along with sound and useful insights were misconceptions and errors of fact or interpretation, surprising from a mature scholar of such large reputation and accomplishment. For example, his calling Erskine "Presbyterian" gives the wrong impression, for when he wrote it was the sole institution of the small Associated Reformed Presbyterian Church, or ARP, a different body from the large Presbyterian Church (USA) with which the college has only recently come to be associated (a dual relationship). He calls Elon "Church of Christ"—a careless error, for it is United Church of Christ, again a quite different denomination. He misinterprets something or other about Webster, Davidson, Ohio Wesleyan, LaVerne, Wake Forest, and many more. A woman's college, he suggests, is for "shy women"; a black college is for "self-mistrustful blacks."[17]

In this article he assumes two types of church-founded schools: (1) institutions in which "faculty members had long since freed themselves from clerical control," and (2) "evangelical colleges," in which presumably the faculty are still under clerical control. He exempts most Catholic colleges from this latter group, as explained in a section entitled "Seculari-zation of the Once-Catholic Colleges." But into this rainbow category of "evangelical" he lumps institutions as diverse as Wake Forest and Brigham Young. When he wrote, the former had been for half a century non-funda-mentalist and "freed from clerical control," though loyally Southern Baptist, and the latter fundamentalist Mormon.[18]

Though noting that they and others in this group "differ very much from one another," he consigns all of them to what he calls "academic and cultural backwaters." As his title shows, they are in his mind "untouched by the academic revolution." Of course these colleges, he concedes, do some good things now and then. Mars Hill, for instance, got a grant for a competence-based program from the Fund for the Improvement of Post-Secondary Education (FIPSE), and Riesman seems surprised. There is, in fact, a slightly patronizing air about his illustrations and his judgments. All of these tail-of-the-procession colleges, as he views them, are fine places for young-sters of limited ability and good manners, who or whose parents seek protection and a highly moral environment.[19]

It may be a lack of information more than of respect. He writes, "Not all evangelical colleges are rural. Birmingham-Southern College, which is United Methodist [he has it right so far], regards itself as Christian in a way that, for example, Ohio Wesleyan, which was begun by Methodists, no longer does." ("Christian"? In what sense? Riesman may mean "church-re-lated," but so is Ohio Wesleyan.) With that strange and shaky judgment Birmingham-Southern (an excellent liberal arts college with Phi Beta Kappa and other distinctions, comparable in many ways with Ohio Wesleyan) is discussed as a prime example of his second-rate category, along with Oral Roberts (non-denominational) and Oklahoma Christian (which *is* Church of Christ). Riesman's concluding sentence about all these institutions is: "The evangelical colleges offer a partial and temporary escape from freedom—an enclave that is neither total nor totalitarian."[20]

About the time *The Academic Revolution* came out in a second or "Phoenix" edition, I was engaged in trying to develop a new way of grouping the mass of church-related institutions, so as to make possible a systematic discussion of their achievements and problems without having to rely on outmoded marks or highly suspect categories. It occurred to me that all such colleges might properly be pictured as strung along a lengthy line, a continuum, separated from each other by only slight degrees of difference in respect to the character of their relationship to their church. If this line were to be put into a chart, the customary travelling of the eye, Western style, would dictate that it run from west to east. Let's not say from left to right, for that would introduce political implications which would lead us astray. The point of the exercise was to call a halt to the game, "I'm more church-related than you are," rather than to add fuel to that hot but unenlightening fire.[21]

Yet such a well-populated continuum needs to be broken up at least slightly, to enable us to denote various positions along the spectrum. So, with apologies for imprecise descriptives, I suggested that those to the west of the line might be called the Embodying Colleges, or Reflections of the Church; those in the center the Proclaiming Colleges, or Witnesses for the Church; and those to the east the Consonant Colleges, or Allies of the Church. But all of them on the spectrum are church-related, even though some on each extreme might not want to recognize such kinship with those on the opposite end.[22]

As we look at this imaginary continuum, we discover that it has movement. Chapter 1, above, took note of the maturing process that went on during the twentieth century, which suggests that any college that was a Reflection of its church in, say, 1910, is likely now to be its Witness or its Ally. The institutional movement runs from more to less rhetoric by the college, from more to less organic tie with the church, from less to more academic achievement. The facts of the colleges' development in this century bear out the directional shifts. But it needs repeating: all the colleges on the line are authentically church-related in the way in which they, but not always their churches or some of their leaders, have come to define such relatedness.[23]

The occasional efforts by demanding churchmen or confused secularists to define the church-related colleges by means of artificial and outmoded plumb lines are losing their steam. The colleges, and increasingly the denominations, now widely recognize the gradations of difference between various institutions, whether along a spectrum or within some other plausible metaphor. We are almost ready to undertake an analysis of the college itself, of the pros and cons of its relationship to some denomination, and of the basic elements in its special nature.

But there is one more voice of misunderstanding and protest to which we must listen. Some of the young neoconservatives in the churches and the academic communities are challenging the ground over which we have come, and it is to their attack on the large majority of the church-related colleges that we now turn.

Chapter Four

Neoconservatives:
Wistful and Assertive

It is probably harder to start a college now than it was a hundred or so years ago, and harder also to kill one. Although the academic heroes of the nineteenth century might well have complained of many hardships, the formalities of starting and ending a college would not be among them. In, say, 1850 to 1875, people of like mind could rally around, find a few students and classrooms, and get something going without a lot of hassle from civil agencies. And if their like-mindedness, their students, or their classrooms gave out, they could just walk away. As the twentieth century winds down, both starting and stopping are more difficult.

So if you and I were ideologues who are disappointed in the present and wistful for the past, and who meant to have a college to our taste, what would we do? If we were mild-mannered, we'd probably deplore what seems to have happened to the institutions we love and once admired, and advocate their repentance and reform. If we were more assertive about the rightness and urgency of our opinions, we might find it expedient today to take over some one or more existing colleges, rather than let them die—or start from scratch. Either way, we'd raise a fuss.

During the latter half of the twentieth century, many old-line church leaders became dispirited about their colleges and largely ineffective in bending them to church control. Many secularists did not help, for their analysis of the church-related institutions was inadequate and led to a dismissive attitude as to their quality. In the two preceding chapters, we have seen that both groups defined such colleges in ways which the institutions themselves had diluted or discarded. As for the colleges, most of them had come to a new maturity and were fully involved in other, mainly academic concerns. Cherishing their relaxed church relationship, they no longer bothered about the outmoded minutiae of the tie—to which we shall give more specific attention in the following chapter.

Longing and Conserving

The time was ripe, then, for religionists of one or another stripe, conscientious about their faith and its acceptance, to register their dismay at what they felt was happening or had already happened to many of the church-related colleges. During the sixties, give or take a few years depending on cultural, denominational, and geographical differences, church leaders with an eye to their campuses began to worry aloud. Dismay was in the air, of course, for that was the time the so-called mainstream churches were forced to recognize their decline in numbers and influence. It seemed not to occur to them that, when much else was in disarray, many of the church-related colleges might actually have been getting stronger.

In any event, commentators often assumed that the colleges were part of the general ecclesiastical decline. The educational historians and philosophers who had been nurtured in mainline churches were of course saddened by this, as they thought, factual development. Other observers, coming from quite different premises—nonbelievers from one angle, conservative evangelicals from another—did not dispute the assumption that the malaise of the old-line denominations was infecting their colleges as well. The churches would not have liked to admit that their colleges were healthier than they themselves.

Distinct from the two earlier groups of critics, the old-line church leaders and the secularists, this third group who seemed to misunderstand much about the church-related colleges began to express themselves in the 'sixties and 'seventies, came to full voice in the 'eighties, and are still at it in the 'nineties. Who are these people? And what has prompted their distress?

First, they seem not to be large in number. A scattering, they are genuinely concerned; on occasion some of them can even be strident. But so far as I can tell, though they have occasionally received a sympathetic hearing, they seem not to have been widely successful in stirring up the colleges.

Yet the colleges may not have given them the attention that they, or at least the thoughtful and constructive ones among them, deserve. These people are not church politicians or secular outsiders. They are men and women of faith, scholars and students of scholarship, who love their colleges but wish they were different, more like the colleges were in the good old days. Or rather, they do not wish the colleges to be throwbacks; they simply want the colleges to face the future with a full appreciation of their rootage in the past.

This third group of commentators are no more of one faith or of one religious conviction than they are of one collegiate loyalty. They defy easy identification by one name. "Evangelical" is not accurate, though some of them are. "Fundamentalist" is name-calling, though some of them are. "Post-this-or-that" is unsatisfactory, because they may or may not be riding a downward curve. "Conservative" by itself is just about as meaningless as "liberal." We need a term, not so much that scholars will approve as that thoughtful lay citizens will understand. So I am calling this amorphous group "neoconservatives," because though somewhat inaccurate, that term is less inaccurate and more innocuous, both blessings, than any other I can think of.

This group is not merely nostalgic, and many of its members are not nostalgic at all. They appreciate the past, to be sure, yet they appreciate, and often produce, a factual and/or critical assessment of it. So far, so good. But a second and more troubling characteristic is that they try to develop a normative account of a church-college relationship, with the church as the axis, or pivot, or fulcrum, and the college as a radiating arm or element.

Theirs is of course a viable position, and for much of the colleges' history it was almost the only angle of vision from which the matter was examined. In recent years, a second group has emerged: those who also want to develop a normative account of a college-church relationship but who do not regard the church as the axis. This second group, to which I adhere, feels that the college rather than the church is and should be the pivotal partner, not because the college was historically the prior factor (for of course it wasn't). Rather, because the college is currently the primary definer and manager of the relationship, and in my view of the desirable tie, ought to be. (I shall develop my own position further in chapter 6.)

The general argument of the neoconservatives is that the church-related colleges have been truer than other colleges in the past to the beliefs they espouse or the supportive behavior they approve. Differences among them are not merely the predictable ones of denominational affiliation, theological orientation, and scholarly maturity, though these grounds for differentiation are abundant and prevent unanimity. The most striking differences within the neoconservative fold are ones of temper. Some are moderate and ready for restrained discourse; some are angry and ready for a fight. Some furl the banner, and give today's style of church-related higher education a premature burial, respectful or not. Some unfurl a new banner, and give their target a considerable beating, deserved or not. But all of them, one way or another, have bought into the old-time indices and base their points of view and prescriptions on the outmoded marks of relatedness that most of the colleges have long since given up.

To examine the arguments in more detail, let us begin where the decibels are low. For several decades the chief officers of the church agencies or boards of education that maintain connections with groups of colleges— Baptist both American and Southern, Catholic, United Church of Christ, Disciples, Episcopal, Lutheran, Methodist, Presbyterian and others—have periodically gathered their faithful institutions to talk about mutual concerns. The smaller denominations with fewer colleges have kept in touch similarly. In nearly all of these conferences and exchanges the church leaders, mostly bound by old definitions, have begun to ask: "Are the colleges true to their rootage and their history? In what sense can they now be said to be church-related? Are they recognizably _____ (fill in the brand name) or maybe 'Christian'? How can you tell?" Let it be noted, these earnest discussions have been mostly amicable though inconclusive.[1]

The statement that caught a wider audience than simply one or another church's solemn assembly turned out to be an article in the *Christian Century* entitled "Are Church-Related Colleges Also Christian Colleges?" The author, Richard G. Hutcheson, Jr., is a Presbyterian minister and church-college trustee who, at the time of writing in 1988, was listed as a "senior fellow" at Richard John Neuhaus's Center on Religion and Society, known as a quite conservative agency. Hutcheson's concern is "the present stance of many mainline church-related colleges," and to the question of whether or not they are "Christian" his answer is nearly always no.[2]

In fact there might be no Christian colleges at all if it weren't for Davis and Elkins, the board of which he recently joined, and which is making "a serious effort to bring together 'church related' and 'Christian' . . . " "Results are far from conclusive." He reports that "at a recent symposium, two former presidents of church colleges listed factors that had characterized such colleges prior to the 1960s"; and then, repeating nearly all the old marks described in chapter 2, above, he concludes correctly, "Little if any of this remains true today. . . . "[3]

Which means, to Hutcheson, that very few can be said to be "Christian." He mentions approvingly Gordon, LeTourneau, Liberty, Messiah, Oral Roberts, and Westmont; Wheaton (the Illinois one, of course) is alluded to three times, and the Christian College Coalition twice; no other institutions are praised. His query is plaintive: "But cannot some church-related colleges offer a distinctively Christian education and atmosphere?"[4]

"Distinctively" supersedes "recognizably" as his favorite modifier for "Christian," but he has difficulty in identifying what the "distinctively Christian dimension" consists in. Many of the old-time churchmen's requirements would apply, of course, but the college would need something more. "At its heart would be the Christian proclamation that there is a sovereign God, incarnate in Jesus Christ and attested by the biblical revelation. . . . "[5] In other words, only an evangelical stance would do, not just for a church but also for a college.

Following the publication of Hutcheson's article, the letters to the editor of the *Christian Century* were probably predictable. Writers from Elmhurst and St. Andrews Presbyterian, both solidly church-related, took opposite views: a) "At last someone has had the courage to speak the truth . . ." (E.); and b) "The tone of Hutcheson's piece—even more than the argument— alerts us to what he is really about . . ." (St. A.P.).[6]

On the *Christian Century's* invitation, F. Thomas Trotter, longtime head of the United Methodist Board of Higher Education and Ministry, and now President of Alaska Pacific, wrote a useful rejoinder, "The College as the Church's Gift," in which he rejected Hutcheson's narrow understanding of "church-related" and "distinctively Christian," and instead portrayed the church-affiliated institution as it is, not as someone wishes it were. But Hutcheson's reply missed Trotter's point; Hutcheson concluded: "It is not necessary to leave the field to the non-church-related, often ultraconservative, and sometimes highly sectarian institutions that dominate the Christian College Coalition. There is a place for distinctively Christian higher education in mainline church-related colleges."[7]

A point of view somewhat similar to Hutcheson's is the thesis of Arthur J. De Jong in his volume of 1990, *Reclaiming a Mission: New Directions for the Church-Related College*. Many of the suggestions therein turned out to be old "directions." De Jong is President of Whitworth, which is Presbyterian (USA) and also a member of the Christian College Coalition. Reviews were not surprising: most favorable from the "evangelicals," and less so from the "liberals." In fact, one reviewer, a trustee of Westminster College, Pennsylvania, tried it both ways, with different reviews in two quite different publications.[8]

Before we leave the quieter levels of debate, a tempting but unsound line of argument by some neoconservatives and perhaps others should be noted.

Accepting the fact of decline among mainline churches, a few commentators have argued that the church-related college is part of the general retreat. When some college doesn't fit that formula, then it must not be sufficiently, or properly, or convincingly church-related. But these notions don't wash. The doomsayers have not made either of the two cases they espouse about the churches' colleges: that such colleges are in decay and/or that the ones that aren't are no longer truly church-related.[9]

Adamant and Aggressive

But some of the neoconservatives try hard to make both cases. They are on the attack, with slashing criticisms of the mainline churches. Not all of one orthodoxy, of course, they affirm a cacophony of positions, come from an array of denominations, and can be expected also to differ along political, economic, and social lines. But they agree on one or two things: the old-guard, established churches have sold out to secularism, and most of their colleges are said to be in even worse shape, conceptually lost to orthodox faith and managerially lost to church control.[10]

Secularization is the summary charge against the colleges. The conviction that the church-related institutions have thrown aside their religious upbringing produces the questions serving as titles for two recent articles, "Is There a Place for Christianity at Duke?" and "Can Notre Dame Be Saved?" The answers were predictably the same: there is no salvation for the Methodist or the Catholic university unless each affirms its religious affiliation in the new old-fashioned way the authors desire.[11]

Each school does affirm its religious affiliation, but the "way the authors desire" turns out to be a helpfully defining phrase for the neoconservative point of view. Those two church-related universities, like many another institution linked to many another denomination, are sufficiently open and tolerant as to allow free expression to widely divergent points of view, even to some that would not allow such liberty to others. But the adamant, aggressive true believers seem not to want merely to be heard; do they want supremacy of, and, from others, consequent subservience to, their own version of ecclesiastical orthodoxy? Their title questions really run: Is there a special place for *my* brand of Christianity at Duke? Can Notre Dame be saved *my* way?

The inventors of those two intriguing queries and their ilk would not be likely to agree with this description. Rather, they would probably say that they are simply trying to restore some balance in the academic discussion, and to persuade the identified institutions to return to their authentic roots in historic Methodism, Catholicism, or whatever other ism they once espoused. But the trouble with that defense is threefold: a) it takes little account of differences in the rootage itself; b) it ignores the possibility—the actuality—of growth and change in the churches' own positions through the years; and c) perhaps most important, it does not recognize the large, demonstrable, maturing change in the relationship of the colleges and universities to their ecclesiastical sponsors during this century.

From a number of illustrations that might be cited, I will confine this exposition to the work of three scholars who are especially thoughtful, and illuminating for the neoconservative point of view. These three, in the order in which their ideas will be discussed, have close ties to the two universities just mentioned: Stanley Hauerwas, once at Notre Dame, now professor at Duke; George Marsden, who moved in 1992 from a Duke to a Notre Dame professorate; and James T. Burtchaell, formerly professor at Notre Dame. It should not be assumed, however, that their universities have succumbed to their argumentation, for that is happily not the case.

Hauerwas teaches in both the Divinity and Law Schools, and writes widely on ethics and related fields. Therefore he comes derivatively to the relationship between church and university, and his two essays on this subject in a recent collection of his writings hit hard. The first, "Truth and Honor: The University and the Church in a Democratic Age," poses the question, "What is the Christian University?" He makes light of what he thinks are the usual answers: "The Christian college is justified because it alone is committed to . . . a liberal arts curriculum . . . is concerned with the 'whole student' . . . or . . . offers value education. . . . " His summary: "In other words, St. Alonzo of the Left Elbow of the Immaculate Conception on the Mount may not be a multiversity . . . and we thank God for it."[12]

Describing "what distinctive character a Christian university should have," Hauerwas asks, ". . . [Do] we have a church that is distinctive enough that it can set priorities and purposes for its universities?" (He does not ask whether it is any longer appropriate for a church to assume such a task.) His answer to the question is "no": "For it is my thesis that the university as an institution that is characterized by the virtues of honor and truthfulness has been undermined by certain democratic values." He leaves the impression that the defining of those virtues and values should be done by the right kind of church.[13]

His second essay that bears on the subject carries the provocative title, "How Christian Universities Contribute to the Corruption of Youth." One way is to forget their original mottoes, such as Harvard's *Veritas: Christo et Ecclesia,* to which Hauerwas adds, *"Veritas* is quite enough challenge for the contemporary university." But, he maintains, "The possibility of being a 'Christian College' still exists at smaller schools that specialize in liberal arts or pre-professional education." The only one he mentions with approval is Anderson, a Church of God institution in Anderson, Indiana.[14]

For a college to become "Christian," Hauerwas would want much more, of course, than the acceptance of outmoded minutiae in management and moral behavior. He longs for "a university that avows Christian identity," which means "to say that certain matters cannot be left out of the conversation. . . ." The answer is that these matters need not be left out, even or especially when the institution enjoys its own autonomy. Yet when it does possess that autonomy, no outside church, not even the school's sponsor, will set the terms for what is included in the college's discourse. Hauerwas sees the dilemma: "I must admit that I think there is no solution to the primary moral issue I have drawn."[15]

Secularism is of course the problem, and secularization is the villain that has brought it about. The neoconservative scholar who has perhaps been most widely engaged in pointing to the evils of secularization is George Marsden, but before examining his position, we should take note of some uses to which that ubiquitous word has been put, and the oft-noted imprecision and slipperiness of its meaning.

It is possible, I suppose, for secularization simply to be factual, and therefore neutral. Fifty or so years ago, in what seems now to have been a less argumentative day, I used the word to denote the reduction or elimination of religion from the college scene; and I reported that whereas secularization was taking place for some aspects of college behavior, for others the movement was actually in reverse. For example, the teaching of religion in regular courses and departments was growing rapidly in all types of institutions, not just those related to some denomination. Other students reported similar findings.[16]

But the term is not merely neutral or factual; oughtness and especially ought-notness soon came to be attached to its use. To those of religious bent it sounds negative, and many churchmen were sure they didn't like it. Others, however, equally loyal to their version of the Christian faith, constructed a positive case for secularization that saw the university as more, not less, open to religion. For example, it was held that secularization actually aided the spread of the teaching of religion; such instruction became available and appealing to more than just the pious.[17]

Times and tastes change. With the growth of evangelicalism and the assertiveness of some of its leaders, most of the institutions of higher education, including a large majority of church-related colleges, are condemned as having sold out to secularism. Marsden is probably the most effective exponent of this point of view. In the 1992 symposium *The Secularization of the Academy,* of which he was the primary editor (and which allows for views other than his own), the first chapter is his definitive statement on "The Soul of the American University."[18]

It is a lost soul, he fears. Once upon a time higher education in this country was largely Protestant. But now, he feels, "almost no distinctively Christian program" remains; "almost no one seems to think that religion is 'very important' for higher education." There are no "major universities that are Protestant in any interesting sense. Protestants do control a fair number of small liberal arts colleges. Those schools that are connected to mainline denominations tend to be influenced only vaguely by Christianity." His only footnote for this position is Richard Hutcheson's article, mentioned above.[19]

The situation, in his view, "is all the more striking, not only because Protestants have forsaken a long tradition of leadership in higher education but also because they have forsaken it so recently and forgotten it so completely." It is "since the 1960s" that the worst of all this has occurred: "Academics" have come to believe that "University education and the intellectual inquiry associated with it, . . . by its very nature excludes religiously informed points of view. To suggest anything else is academic heresy."[20]

But what are "religiously informed points of view"? His only? And, for that matter, what does he mean, "excludes"? He speaks his mind openly and freely. Clearly, he wants more than he has got, and equally clearly, he thinks he won't get it. His foregoing sentiments preface a lengthy, carefully constructed argument about why higher education is secular—"the demands of a technological society," "ideological conflicts," and "cultural pluralism"—and how all those things have led to "collapse and confusion." "Despite the presence of many religion departments . . . religion has moved from near the center a century or so ago to the incidental periphery . . . about as important as the baseball team." "It is not neglected, but its unique perspectives, especially those of traditional Christianity, are often excluded and even ridiculed."[21]

In his final section, "Prescription," Marsden points out that "two major strategies are available" to those who, he feels, "are seriously Christian." "The first is for seriously religious people to begin to campaign actively for universities to apply their professions of pluralism more consistently." In other words, to let the evangelicals and fundamentalists back into the campus colloquy. "The second strategy, which may be more realistic, is for serious Christians to concentrate on building distinctly Christian institutions that will provide alternatives to secular colleges and universities."[22]

When one recalls the evangelical weight that Marsden gives to such words as "seriously" and "distinctly Christian," it becomes clear why he casts into outer darkness most of the church-related colleges of the present time. He complains understandably (and justifiably, in some cases) that the field is tilted against him. His stature as a scholar gives assurance that he truly wants a level playing field. But would the college he desires be an academic home for any except those of his particular persuasion?

Moreover, his commentary reads as if he thought of himself as spokesman more for the church than for the college. This is, of course, his choice, and he has every right to make it. If he and his fellow neoconservatives want to bend church-related colleges to their particular theory and practice, they have full liberty to try to do so. But they need to guard against the extravagant claim that only those colleges allowing themselves to be bent in their direction deserve the designation of church-related, and that all others are derelict.

The Alleged Villainy at Vanderbilt

One more thing they should be careful about is not to fudge the facts in an effort to construct their case. The most mischievous and deplorable example I know is the two-part essay by James T. Burtchaell entitled "The Decline and Fall of the Christian College," which appeared in early issues of Richard John Neuhaus's conservative journal of opinion, *First Things*. His earlier title for the manuscript had even more bite: "The Drift into Secularization of Christian Higher Education in America: An Autopsy."[23]

Burtchaell began by noting the large numbers of colleges founded by churches, and moved quickly to his theme that "There has been, from earliest times, a tendency towards alienation." (The word in his first draft was "secularization," but that was not sharp enough.) Colleges pulled away, the Catholic ones being "the last great cohort to be drawn into the process." But secularization (this time he used the word) "is not complete": he took heart from "the small and culturally withdrawn colleges with a campus ethos strongly enough at variance with the dogmas and dictates of Modern Scholarship to disdain and resist it thus far. . . ." He mentioned five as fitting this category: "Wheaton, Liberty, Oral Roberts, Calvin, Goshen"; but though all are safely evangelical, the first three are not related to a particular denomination.[24]

"Perhaps the trend is inexorable. . . . Whether or not emancipation from church be the necessary condition or the inevitable result of intellectual excellence, it behooves us to understand the history and the elemental structure of this secularization." Burtchaell proposed to study "an archetypical case," namely, Vanderbilt University, during roughly the last quarter of the nineteenth century and up to its final break with the Methodist Episcopal Church, South, in 1914. That was inviting for him, because a massive and remarkably objective history of Vanderbilt had recently been published. Burtchaell hoped to "disengage a pattern from that story" in order "to venture a hypothetical model of the process."[25]

Those who have read Paul Conkin's history, *Gone with the Ivy,* and/or know the Vanderbilt story from other sources, will recognize that Burtchaell's effort was not successful. He misused Conkin's book in order to construct a seriously flawed interpretation. His account included:

—faulty descriptions of governance and custom at the University;
—inaccurate characterizations of chief protagonists, such as the University Chancellor and various bishops;
—a biased record of events, with omissions; and
—misunderstandings of campus and community life.[26]

Burtchaell made it appear that the Chancellor, James H. Kirkland, was the "devious" mastermind of the complete break from the Church, and that loyal churchmen were solidly against him; but neither claim squares with the facts. Even the bishops were not unanimously opposed to the break, and all the way along the University had strong support from alumni, other Methodist colleges, and a broad spectrum of the Church. The decisive vote in the Southern Methodists' General Conference of 1914, which sealed the separation, was by the close margin of 150 to 140, but it would have hurt

Burtchaell's case to have mentioned it. Perhaps his errors should be excused because neither he nor Conkin was there. But my father was (and I was too, from 1911 on), and from his chair of religious education in the seminary he witnessed the dispute close at hand. To any who know the true story, the case for the villainy of Vanderbilt against the Church falls flat.[27]

From his misreading of "the basic elements of the Vanderbilt experience," to which he added "suggestive parallels to be found in the wider Protestant experience," Burtchaell drew up nine propositions to explain to his satisfaction what has happened to church-related higher education in general. All nine were predicated on the unspoken assumption that the church ought to define, manage, and control the college. Key features of his position, with sound, unsound, and preposterous ideas all mixed together (and with my reactions in parentheses) ran as follows:

"First, . . . stagnation . . . Then . . . intellectual turbulence. . . . Spokesmen for the Church's concerns, by a compound of incapacity and animosity, exacerbated the apparent hostility between the church and rigorous scholarship." (A nugget of truth, but overdrawn, even for 1900, VU and elsewhere.)

"Second, there was a president . . . who saw the ecclesiastical establishment as a real or potential adversary to his project and rival to his power." (It would be as true, for Vanderbilt and many another, if the sentence were turned around. Time and again, some segments of the church would see the president as an adversary to *its* power.)

"Third, the estrangement from sponsoring church occurred at a time when the funding the church may have provided was clearly inadequate. . . . " (Yes, you can say that again.)

"Fourth, there was a transfer of primary loyalty from the church to the 'academic guild,' especially on the part of the faculty." (Here B. began a series of sweeping assertions to which the only sound reaction has to be yes-and-no. It was not true that "the Vanderbilt academics preferred to dissociate themselves from their religious leaders," but the colleges were indeed deciding some things for themselves.)

"Fifth, erosion of the will to consider active communion in the church . . . extinguished the university's ability to consider itself a unit of the church." (B then started to show his full hand: "active communion" has to do with how many communicants—in Vandy's case, Methodists—were in the student body, faculty, deanships, etc. He was looking for old-style marks of identification and couldn't find them.)

"Sixth, there was a progressive devolution of church-identifiers: first from Methodist to generically Christian, then to generically religious, then to flatly secular." (To be sure, there was a shift in self-conception by Vanderbilt and other colleges, but not as sharp or antireligious as B. maintains. His use of "church-identifiers" makes clear that only church control would do.)

"Seventh, in its anxiety to appeal to one constituency . . . while not antagonizing another . . . , the academy replaced its religious identity with reductionist equivalents." (It was, of course, a neoconservative's definition of "religious identity" that had lost ground, and those "reductionist equivalents" turned out to be "moral character . . . as a substitute for Christian faith and community. . . ." In fact, he held that "The moral equivalencies . . . [are] secular surrogates for sacred convictions and commitments.")

"Eighth, theological studies . . . were set apart from the academic center . . . a banishment into marginality." (B.'s picture was not true for Vanderbilt and many other places.)

"Ninth, it has been active Christians, not hostile secularists, who were most effective in alienating the colleges and universities from their communities of faith." (Well, well. But not the "active Christians" B. approved of.)[28]

At this point Burtchaell moved to Part II of his argument. Since he maintained that "the Vanderbilt transition from Methodist to neuter exhibits a typical pattern of academic secularization," he furnished unnamed examples of universities A, B, C, D, E, and F that, in his view, were on the downward path. The capitals were faint disguises, and perhaps meant to be. For example, the indiscretion at "D _____ University" took place, he said, "at a spot within sight of the campus chapel and almost within the ambit of the founder's bronze statue . . ." What's your guess? If my hunches are correct as to the institutions he coyly referred to, Burtchaell was as inaccurate in describing Duke's and others' church relationships as he was in telling the Vanderbilt story.[29]

The same defection was now going on, he felt, in Catholic institutions. His "pastiche of contemporary anecdotes," as he called them, came from the Catholic campuses of G, H, I, and J. (V, W, X, Y, and Z were used for various supporting entities, to keep us guessing.) All this led to the five concluding "morals to the story," which seemed to be a last-gasp effort to save "the Christian College," both Catholic and Protestant, from "The Decline and Fall" to which he felt it had already succumbed. I agree wholeheartedly with his fifth "moral": "Lastly, whatever a university or college is committed to must be able to be professed out loud, and honestly. . . ."[30]

But three of the other four showed what Burtchaell really wanted, and the fourth what he expected:

"1. The only plausible way for a college or university to be significantly Christian is for it to function as a congregation in active communion within a church. . . .

"2. In every one of its component elements—governors, administrators, faculty, and students—the academy must have a predominance of committed and articulate communicants of its mother church. . . .

"3. A Christian college or university must advise noncommunicant members openly and explicitly when welcoming them that the institution is constitutionally committed to its church in a way that must transcend and transfigure the commitments of individual members. . . .

"4. Granted the inveterate intellectual mediocrity within the churches and their officers, and the inveterate contempt for faith among intellectual elites, the Christian college or university must expect continual low-intensity distrust from either direction. . . ."[31]

Is it any wonder that the church-related colleges by and large have rejected the locksteps that Burtchaell and to a lesser extent other neoconservatives have advocated? Variously orthodox and evangelical, they cannot shape the colleges to their will, for the colleges have grown beyond them in exercising their own autonomy and making their own programmatic decisions. Neoconservatives do not succeed in blaming this or that institution, this or that president, unless they twist the facts, and that doesn't work. They are as devoted to the old indices of what church relationship ought to mean as the controlling churchmen or the dismissive secularists were in days gone by. And the tactic of reading the church-related colleges out of court, of condemning them as unchristian when they don't believe or behave as the neoconservatives prescribe, is not likely to last much longer either.

So let us move on, as the colleges themselves have moved on, to look more closely at who they are and what they have become. In the following chapter we shall take note of the manifold ways in which the institutions founded by denominations have continued to be related to them in both discord and harmony.

Chapter Five

Discord and Harmony

Colleges sometimes misbehave.

And so, of course, do churches.

In fact, it is probably correct to say that every collection of human beings misbehaves at some time or other—begging the question as to what misbehavior consists in and who does the judging. It is in the group genes.

Good behavior too is ubiquitous. "Snafu" ought to have a proper companion acronym: "snaww"—situation normal, all working well. Our primary attention in this chapter is directed to colleges and their kind, and to prove how partial I am, let it here be argued that higher education, totally and in its manifold parts, sometimes does things right. The institutions that are related one way or another to some ecclesiastical body need to be included in such a sweeping judgment.

But since we are looking here not at such colleges in toto but only pointedly at their relationships with one or another church, their good and less-than-good behavior, and the good and less-than-good reasons for it, will have to do primarily with the ways the colleges and the churches get along together.

How do they get along? The expected—and true—answer is, sometimes well, sometimes ill. Discord and harmony are both present, and may be taken as the two poles of a relationship that is both lively and still holding together. If the bond goes beyond discord into irreconcilable conflict, the end is near. If it goes beyond harmony into loss of distinct identity for the college, the end is also near. But the great body of contact is somewhere between the two poles, and episodes of relationship are usually softer, lowercase versions of discord and of harmony. Whatever the degrees of feeling, it is important to ask what they consist in and why.

The Colleges as They Are

The first step, I think, is to be more specific than I have been thus far about the precise identifications of the church institutions. A systematic and somewhat philosophical definition of the nature of a genuine church-related college must wait until the next chapter, but let us note now the rough lineaments and boundaries of the breed. The mythical constructs of old-time churchmen, poorly informed secularists, and party-line neoconservatives have failed us. But the questions as to who and what the colleges really are still stand.

Earlier on, I offered the opinion that nobody knows how many church-related colleges there are. But there is somebody who comes close to knowing: my colleague, Joan Keeton Young, deserves high marks for her compilation in Appendices A and B. Take a break to look at them; and let us know whether you agree, or where you might want to make amendments.

The awkward problem of identifying church-related colleges may be worse now than it has ever been. Over fifty years ago I tackled it, thinking it was simple. Over thirty years ago I did it again, knowing it was a deceptive query. "Whether or not a college is church-related depends partly on who is answering the question." It also depends on who is "doing the asking"; and having thus tied myself in knots, I got out as best I could.[1]

Nowadays the difficulty is laughable. Who is answering the question and who is doing the asking are only two of the amusing variables; audience, and time, place, and circumstance can all affect the outcomes. The National Council of Churches, the *World Almanac,* the Association of American Colleges, the *Directory of Higher Education,* the individual denominational lists, all say different things. It has become so bad that the *Yearbook of American and Canadian Churches,* which used to try to report college affiliations, gave up in 1992: they knew there were too many uncertainties.[2]

On a hunch I dropped by the office of a large church-college association and asked the person in charge, "Have you a reliable list of your denomination's colleges?" "Oh, yes," and he gave me a printed brochure. "But," I said, "there seem to be one or two missing." "Well, a few are so poor they find it hard to pay the modest dues. And the association is thought to be too liberal or too conservative for others. What you have is the official list." Yet when he understood why I wanted to know, he was very helpful. He got typed up for me the names of the "nonmembers" of his association, equivalent to over 10 percent of the membership.

Appendix A is the *unofficial* list, composed of both members and non-members. It includes nearly all the names that have always appeared in such lists and a few that are unaccustomed to being seen in such company. It does not knowingly include either the dead or the yet-unborn. The alphabetical roll-call by colleges is followed by the church groupings in Appendix B, both those related to the larger or at least the college-rich denominations, and those others with small membership or number of affiliates. All the colleges are listed in both ways, by alphabet and by church, though the total for the second is a bit larger than for the first because some colleges are related to more than one denomination. These appendices were pretty reliable the day they were put on the computer, and they will continue to be almost accurate, probably more so than any other list you can find, for, I daresay, a few months.

Hold you finger at Appendix B for another moment, please. The grouping by families—"other" Baptist or Methodist or whatever—is more to save space than to note cooperation. Colleges of all types do cooperate with each other, of course, in all sorts of consortia, and many churches are indeed ecumenically active. But church-college associations seldom look with favor upon spreading their seminars wide enough to take in outside colleges, even those presumably close to their party line.

A case or two in point: when the Northern and Southern Presbyterian colleges were getting together, I made so bold as to suggest that they invite a couple of colleges affiliated with small "Presbyterian" denominations to join them, but to no avail. (Ten years later I noticed that Erskine is now listed as Presbyterian USA as well as ARP. So far, so good.) Once I inquired as to whether the Methodists might reach out to allow the two Moravian colleges—one simply called Moravian and the other Salem (N.C.)—to join in their useful intercollege meetings. After all, it was among Moravians that John Wesley's heart had been "strangely warmed." But again, my query fell on deaf ears. Yet not all institutions that seem to be eligible can easily be included; Asbury, for example, more Methodist than Mr. Wesley, would probably be uncomfortable.

As for inclusion in the listing of church-related colleges as a whole, I once thought I could see a clear line. In 1961, my opinion was that "if a college says it is not church-related, then that is a pretty clear indication that it is not, no matter what some denominational agency may claim."[3]

But this may no longer be true. There are, sad to say, a few colleges named in Appendices A and B that may not want to confess their church relationship to everybody, if they see a danger in their being thought to be allied with the right wing of their church's membership. This is the reverse side of what was noted as a tendency among some neoconservatives, to rule out of order those colleges that did not conform to their strict requirements.

The tit-for-tat phenomenon may also be present here. That is, there may be a few colleges unwilling to be identified as related to a specific church that is thought by the college to be too liberal—oh, yes, it can happen. Those colleges' names, however, will probably be listed in some other ecclesiastical category rather than being dropped out of the list altogether. At the extremes, the strategies seem to differ: the extreme conservative colleges burrow in; the extreme liberal ones fly the coop. It is in the nature of each position.

We need to recognize, further, that the universe of church-related institutions of higher education—colleges mostly, including two-year ones, but also a goodly number of research universities, a plethora of theological seminaries, both free-standing and not, and a handful of specialized professional institutions—is so polyglot as to be almost impossible to catalogue. Listings are both impenetrable and necessary; we can't rely on them and we can't do without them. We can't generalize about them, except in the vaguest terms or on some historical criteria, probably debatable.

Usually we cannot generalize safely about even their groups and subgroups. Not all Methodist institutions are alike; not all Methodist institutions in the South or the Midwest are alike. Not all Catholic institutions are alike; not all Jesuit institutions are alike. As far as I know, not all colleges of the Church of the New Jerusalem are alike. (That's a joke; there is only one, the Academy of the New Church.)

Yes, but many institutions are remarkably alike across ecclesiastical boundaries. Some Presbyterian schools are quite close to some American Baptist ones, are indistinguishable from United Church of Christ ones, are recognizably kin to some Disciples ones, and so forth. This is the way it really ought to be, at least as far as the colleges rather than the churches are concerned.

Moreover, as the years pass this is coming more and more to be so. With respect to all the larger denominations, and even some of the smaller ones, the typical college (which doesn't exist) of one church is more like the typical college (ditto) of other churches than it is to a typical institution of its own supposedly homogeneous brand. The totality is a smorgasbord, to be sure, but is also narrowing in some respects: across denominational lines colleges are facing many similar problems. Aware that these problems are much the same, and sensing a community with other colleges long thought to differ from them, they are inevitably coming closer together.[4]

All the colleges of Appendices A and B have various kinds of contact with their sponsoring denominations. Between the colleges and the churches are hundreds, thousands, of examples of both concord and discord, and we shall inquire into the nature of both. Names will be given now and then, when the situations have long since become common knowledge. But this discussion is not a gossip factory or a hall of heroes; our interest is in the sources of stress and the grounds for harmony, not primarily the obstreperous or the compliant. That way, we may have less fun but learn more.

Sources of Discord

First, then, for a true story about a college that shall here be nameless. It is the one cherished chick of a smallish denomination, whose governing body has always taken a keen interest in the institution's affairs. Less than twenty years ago—in other words, fairly recently but not in today's headlines—a delegate arose to complain that awful things were going on up at their college: dancing, drinking, drugs, general deviltry. The delegates got sufficiently excited to pass a resolution asking the college to get rid of the culprits.

Whereupon one of the elder statesmen arose and opined, "Much worse things than even this deplorable misbehavior are going on. I have been informed that two members of our Bible Department do not believe in literal inerrancy." This was so shocking that the group became thoroughly aroused, and passed a directive to the college to get rid of those two faculty members, tenured or not.

The next day on the campus three indignant meetings were held and three statements duly issued. The first was the Bible Department, more than two in number, for courses in religion were required. Their statement pointed out that no member of their group believed in literal inerrancy; it was a heresy, and an absurd position for a respectable scholar to take. The second meeting was the faculty as a whole; their statement argued that the church body's action was an invasion of the hallowed principle of academic freedom, to which the college had been faithful for a hundred and fifty years.

Finally, of course, was a special meeting of the trustees. They did not flinch from what they had to say, which ran to this wise: "Though some of us have been elected by the church, once we were chosen, the responsibility for governing this institution was in our hands; and we insist on keeping it there." The church's governing body had to call a session the next day to undo its mischief.[5]

The problems of relationships between a college and its sponsoring denomination are seldom single, but almost never do they crop up in such multitude on one day. Student morals, biblical interpretation, academic freedom, continuing education of a constituency, institutional autonomy—these and more were at stake. To other campuses some of these strains might seem niggling, or on the other hand catastrophic and irreconcilable. But the important thing to recognize is that this kind of basic misunderstanding, of crucial discord, has taken place at almost every church-related college at some time or other and may take place again. The potential sources of discord require explicit elucidation, and every campus needs to be alert.

Every church also needs to be aware. The fact is, the pressures of a parent denomination on its collegiate offspring can often seem unrelenting, and on occasion be quite severe. The reverse proposition does not appear to be so serious: the pressures of a college on its affiliated church are almost never as forceful, in fact seem seldom to take place. But whichever body first gives or receives the pressure is not the point. Rather, it is that, however induced, the stresses and strains of a college-church relationship deserve more notice than they commonly receive, except when a situation explodes into crisis.

Before we examine the chief sources of discord one by one, a word of caution against a tempting but false conclusion is in order. The successful church-related college—successful, that is, in its relationship to its church—is not the college that is always in harmony with its denomination. That really is not possible, unless the college is completely subservient. The successful church-related college is the one that faces up to the strains in its relationship with the church and overcomes them.

The major sources of discord are at least seven. They overlap, of course, and other types may arise from time to time.[6] They have different priorities among the colleges as well as among the churches, and within any college on different occasions; but all can be, and have been, disruptive. At the end of each grouping of complaints I will throw in a few remarks (parenthetically) as to how each has been or might be relieved.

1. The first large strain-producer is the heart of the collegiate enterprise, the area of *academic life*. Churches, no matter how few or many colleges they sponsor, include in their laity, and even clergy, people who are distrustful of assumed expertise and suspicious of eggheads. Now and again

a college will achieve such academic standing as to prompt the question, Does the church really want and welcome an institution of high quality? My own experience, I think, is not unusual. Having been on the faculty or staff of half a dozen church-related institutions, affiliated with four different denominations, I found that such a question was raised by all but one of those constituencies.

This academic stress takes a wide range of forms. Sometimes the problem is the content of the curriculum: there is hardly a subject now alive that somebody somewhere doesn't like, or considers too esoteric (often) or too frivolous (rare). Sometimes the trouble is with the high standard of course work expected, or a requirement that is too rigid. Seldom is the supposed lack of quality a complaint: "Why doesn't our college have a Phi Beta Kappa chapter?" In fact, seldom do the churches, any more than the states or other sponsors, criticize their colleges for not being good enough.

Strangely, no contradiction is seen when the persons who receive the largest acclaim from or for the college also draw the fiercest arrows. The teachers, to be sure, are the ones responsible for the academic life, and they are held accountable. Like other kinds of college, nearly every church college has its famous instance of some professional scalawag, who may in fact have been a hero or a saint, but/and still caused trouble.

Which brings us to the thorny topic of academic freedom and its step-child, tenure. At any one time church colleges as well as state institutions may be listed as having earned the disapproval of the American Association of University Professors; the written accounts are sometimes filled with wrath-venting toward some perpetrator or victim in the academic arena. Actually, church-related colleges have a pretty good record on this matter, although not perfect, and I believe the record is getting better. But in individual cases the church (like the legislature for state schools) has had to be prompted to support the principle of academic freedom.[7]

(What can the college do? It can explain the shape of its academic program in content, method, and personnel, the what and the why. It can strike common cause with all sorts of other colleges. It can step up its effort to educate the public. And it can realize that some will never agree.)

2. The second source of considerable stress is *campus life*. Let us save for later the ills and issues that afflict society at large; the reference now is the supposedly lesser problems raised by campus occurrences—episodic, annoying, photogenic, inflammatory. In respect to social mores, the church

is usually more conservative than the campus, thus more likely to produce tut-tuts, knee-jerk reactions, and generational discord.

Opprobrious items of the not-so-distant past were dancing and drinking. Currently we oldsters get upset by drugs, sex, fraternity shenanigans, and worse. The colleges are tarnished by serious misbehavior in athletics, or by cheating in classroom and laboratory, or by racial confrontations and inequities in group and individual treatment. The list is legion; and the church, as would be true for any other adult entity dealing with adolescent behavior, is not going to like a lot of it. In fact, because it is the church, it may like it a lot less.[8]

(Can the colleges do anything to blunt the effect of adverse campus behavior? First, they can try to catch the trouble early, not to let it fester. Secondly, they can strike a happy medium of concern, between pooh-poohing and viewing as a life-and-death crisis. The off-campus world is bound to react negatively to what happens sometimes on any campus, for these are our young people, and their misbehavior would probably take place also at home. The college must face the situation; on occasion the church's outrage will be justified.)

3. The third area of potential sturm-und-drang has to do with *ideological orthodoxy,* which is a far cry from the previous item. When a church and a college get out of philosophical or theological kilter with each other, it is seldom because the college is too orthodox or fundamentalist or otherwise rigid. Rather, it is nearly always because the college is seen by the church as not being sufficiently conservative in religion, or politics, or biology, or what-have-you.

This is not merely potential; it happens all the time. A half century or more ago, some liberals thought that for reputable colleges, universities, and seminaries, most of these battles were over. But the numbers of new institutions founded in this century by fast-growing evangelical sects are evidence of their desire for theological correctness in the colleges. The recent scuffles among Southern Baptists and Roman Catholics, to name only the two most publicized combatants, demonstrate how demands for adherence to or deliverance from earlier orthodoxies can still generate more heat than light.[9]

(When a church attacks one of its colleges for not being firm in the faith—the exact opposite is much harder to imagine—the college must mount an intensive educational campaign to make its position clear. Being the kind of institution it is, the college cannot be neutral about learning versus ignorance or free inquiry versus indoctrination. If the situation is otherwise, though the institution may still want to be related to its church, it no longer wants really to be a college.)

4. The fourth area of stress and strain that sometimes disrupts the happy relationship between college and church is the world of *social problems* at the doorstep of both institutions. Once again we touch on the liberal-conversative equation, as inadequate as each descriptive tends to be; and one must strive not to pigeonhole or categorize unfairly. Plenty of churches and their leaders are liberal, whatever that means, and plenty of campus types are not. But on balance it remains true that, when or if churchmen and academicians differ on the pressing social issues of our time, the colleges are more likely and the churches less likely to opt for change. And if change proves to be the order of the day, the colleges will probably move first.

Take white-black racism as perhaps the most contentious and riot-prone problem of our time. Little credit can go to either institution for having taken risks on behalf of civil rights, but there is a difference: to this day the churches remain largely homogeneous, while the colleges did desegregate, grudgingly. The churches and their colleges were on separate timetables and seldom employed the same strategies. Pain was sure to follow.

As long-time participants in this particular struggle, my wife and I have often observed how easily the campus charges the church with being spineless, and how readily the congregation accuses the college of being extremist. Some rifts have been deep and slow to heal. In any event, neither the church nor the college can simply walk away from the traumas of its time and place—racism, or poverty, or homelessness, or war, or any of the thousand ills that societies are heir to. If either a church or a college tries to escape, it spells disaster for their kinship, as well as for much else that each says it stands for.[10]

(What can a college do, when some social conviction it espouses is out of line with and distressing to its parent church? It has to tell what it is doing, and more important, why. And it may not win. On occasion, a college must be prepared to lose some support because of a societal stand it feels it must take.)

5. The fifth item is *leadership*. Strange, you may think, that this could be listed as a major cause for conflict between a college and its sponsor, but the unhappy fact is that it is often the operative though hidden element when other reasons are cited. Sometimes the strains are not so much conceptual (e.g., orthodoxy) or behavioral (e.g., campus life) as simply personal.

The story of how the Southern Methodists "lost" Vanderbilt many years ago, already noted in chapter 4, is a case in point. The effort of a contemporary right-wing ideologue to paint Chancellor Kirkland as the villain in the divorce was, as we saw, misguided, but personal distaste between the leaders of college and church was clearly influential. Nobody got shot, for by that time dueling between gentlemen was illegal, but plenty of people got mad.[11]

This is not as frivolous a cause for annoyance as those words might suggest. Now and again the two types of institutions want—and need—different kinds of leaders. They use, and sometimes misuse, different processes of selecting leadership. A good president does not necessarily make a good bishop, and vice versa; and the paths of upward climb leading to the two executive offices are usually quite different. Stylistically, the exercise of ecclesiastical leadership tends to be, but with exceptions, hierarchical; of academic leadership, but also with many exceptions, collegial. Even in the same denomination, the daily routines of the two institutions, campus and congregation, simply don't look alike and work alike. No wonder then that, since different tasks take different kinds of people, the leaders of college and church sometimes get crossed up with one another.[12]

(What to do? Counsel with leaders already aboard, of course, and choose carefully to fill vacancies, so that when issues arise they won't be decided on personality quirks. No matter how they got there, the farmers and the cowboys should be friends.)

6. Sixth in the list is the one that might well have been noted first, for in a college's daily functioning it comes quickest to mind—*support*. I don't know of any instance in which too much support was the cause of strain between a church and one of its educational institutions; it always seems that the support is too little. Moreover, the sustenance a college requires is not financial alone; it needs the time and energy of its partisans as well as money. Help in the recruitment of students; understanding, even forgiveness, when problems arise and generate bad publicity; intangible, psychological, spiritual support—these are the things that when absent cause trouble, when present produce fruitful relationships.[13]

Once upon a time my wife Whitty and I, already retired, went to a lovely church school for a three-year tour of duty, to help tide it over a hump. It was Salem College, in Winston-Salem, an institution related to the Moravians for over two hundred years. One day the church administrator asked me, "What do you think of the support the church gives the college?" I said,

"You mean the $15,000 per year?"—for that was all. When he said, "Yes," I replied, "Well, I've been here too short a time to be sure, but I do know this, it's either too much or too little."

It was, of course, too little to matter greatly to the college budget, and any amount would have been too much were the aim to buy one's way in. But if we had been talking about something other than money, we both would have gladly affirmed the sense of caring that the Moravians had long felt for Salem. Support of whatever kind is a grave issue only when it is absent.

(The wise advice about getting money from a church is, don't count on it. Give up the notion that the church will provide the college with big money, or large numbers of students. The college may indeed get both from church people, but the church per se is not again likely to be a source of large tangible support.)

7. To this point we have considered six possible areas in which stresses and strains can develop between a college and a church: the academic program, the campus life, ideological orthodoxy, problems in society, leadership, and not least, kind and level of support. It may come as something of a shock to realize that these six causes of discord are simply the proximate reasons, the sparks that may set something else aflame. But the seventh is often the basic or definitive reason, the fire itself.

This last item in our listing is *governance*. When discord corrodes the relationship, the fundamental reason may be a mutual *desire for power and control,* an effort to capture or recapture the making of governing decisions for the college. Notice here the emergence of double responsibility for the falling-out: the college may want to capture a power it has never had, and/or the church may strive to recapture a control it has lost.

The former is less likely than ever before to be true, for during the twentieth century, as we have seen, colleges of all sorts have already taken on most or all of the tasks that constitute autonomy. It is the latter, the effort of the church to regain its controlling position, that is the more likely manifestation today. But whatever the issue's point of origin, the substance of the effort is to possess the power to make the major governing decisions for the college.

For example: someone or some group in the church may make a bid for control by attacking the offbeat theological position of a professor, or the palpable misbehavior of a student, or anything that may seem vulnerable. In fact, the real effort is not always so masked; it can be direct as well as circuitous. The play for power, visible or not, may not always be polite; at least figuratively speaking, it can be bloody. But if the illustration that comes quickest to mind in recent days is the Southern Baptist Convention, we should take it at least partly off the hook: other churches have also behaved this way from time to time and will probably do so again.

The parallel with what sometimes takes place between state legislatures and public universities can be both reassuring and depressing. The state and its tax-supported institutions of higher education may experience much the same pattern of stress and strain that the church and its institutions go through, with variations for the differing postures of moral outrage that produce or respond to the outbursts. Similarities are still found in such customs as visiting speakers, both unpatriotic and unpietistic; in student hijinks; in faculty oaths, both loyal and disloyal; in almost anything that takes place on a lively campus. Whatever the event and whatever the type of school, church-related or state-related (and independent of either church or state, for that matter), the college and its sponsor can on occasion find themselves at sad cross-purposes in respect to who is in charge.[14]

(The parenthetical word for this form of discord previews an emphasis of the next chapter: parallel to a recognition of the church's own autonomy needs to be an insistence on the college's possession of its autonomy, even when it may make mistakes.)

As we come to the end of enumerating the strains, call to mind, if you will, the little story with which this section began, about the campus where three meetings were held the same day to undo the church's invasion of the day before. Who was the hero? The hero, I submit, was the college collectively—those who were faithful to their scholarship, who resisted the assault on academic freedom, and who adhered to their duty to govern. And let us not forget, even the churchmen who caused the ruckus played an indispensable part in the happy outcome: they met again to accept the college's position. All of which leads this negatively phrased section into an affirmative conclusion, as follows.

Grounds for Concord

The other side of the college-church relationship, the side not heretofore discussed, is the pleasant and fruitful picture. Constructive and mutually supportive contacts between college and church abound. It is not true to the actual situation to let it appear that discord always outweighs or outnumbers concord. The reverse proposition would be much closer to the truth.

Then why spend so much time on stress and strain? Simply because two people walking along together, or even climbing a difficult slope, never attract the crowd they would draw if they get into a fight. Two harmonious institutions singing in concert are doing what is expected, but let one of them change key and the surrounding air is disturbed. The former associations can move along without a murmur, or a morsel of outside attention, for years on end; but the latter associations can garner unhappy publicity in a wink.

As I look back on time spent in church-related institutions, I believe that sense of common cause was almost always stronger than dissonance. Surely it was true of Scarritt, as I watched my father's presidency from 1921 to 1943. There were plenty of problems, and many occasions when the church was uneasy about the college's frontline conscience on social issues of the day. But the prevailing character of that relationship was mutual appreciation.[15]

I could illustrate, I think, from three places where my wife and I worked during the 'forties—Emory and Henry, Denison, and Pomona—sprung from three different churches and in different parts of the country, but mostly solving problems of their church relationship to their satisfaction. This remains true even though fifty years later the latter two are no longer listed as church-related. Our experience is no more or less instructive than others' of comparable length and variety. But it was ours, and therein lie its credibility and appeal for us. Colleges and churches more often get along, we feel, than not.

Our most intense experience of this congruence of interests was a nine-year tour of duty from 1951 to 1960 at Southern Methodist University and its constituent Perkins School of Theology. We had a front-row seat for every relational crisis between SMU/PST and the Methodist Church (as it was called then), and those two familial institutions both suffered and enjoyed plenty of heart-stopping moments. What we learned was this: the values that bound the University and the Church together during that time, though not as raucous or photogenic as the issues that now and again divided them, proved to be more deeply rooted, more faithful to the essence of each institution, and more long-lasting.

The divisive factors in the SMU situation could serve as examples for every one of the seven causes of discord noted above, with several left over for good measure. But the qualities and verities that both the University and the Church cherished proved stronger. Postponing the discussion of such values to the next chapter, we note now that, though not always practiced, they were always affirmed and consciously shared.[16]

Intimate contacts with other church-related institutions since 1960 have led me, with only one or two exceptions, to the same conclusion. Because of my duties with Danforth and other foundations and, especially since retirement, with short-term consultancies, I've come to know fairly well, at least at the moments of my close contact, a host of such colleges across the country. Among the following, the question of relationship with parent church arose: Alaska Pacific, Allegheny, Austin, Birmingham-Southern, Catawba, Clark Atlanta, Cumberland (TN), Denver, Erskine, Hobart, Huntington, Manchester, Maryville (MO), Randolph-Macon Woman's, Rockhurst, St. Louis University, Salem (NC), Stetson, Wake Forest, Warren Wilson, Wesleyan (GA), Wooster, and some others.

In only two of these colleges did the cons of immediate annoyance seem to outweigh the pros of longtime amity. Since my time of contact, the bond appears to have broken for one of them, but the other institution is back in its church's fold. The prevailing temper for this group, therefore, is that across ecclesiastical lines, the cooling water of continuity is thicker than the hot blood of episodic dispute. Note that the twenty-two colleges named above had eleven different church attachments.[17]

Then are relationships getting better across the board? I'm not sure. Perhaps. At least for most of the colleges, if not as much so for the churches, I think the answer is Yes.

The history of the relationship and the kinds of strains make more likely that the church will get upset sooner and remain upset longer. More likely in some denominations than in others, of course, but more likely in general as well. Except for the relatively few institutions that remain captives of their churches in either management or atmosphere, the large majority of church-related colleges today are independent in spirit, and go about their academic business without what they sometimes view as oppressive piety. It is usually left to the denomination to take umbrage at something the college has said, sponsored, or let happen; often the campus seems to care less.

But the campus does care to have a harmonious relationship with its church, even when it fails to take as seriously as its church does each threat to harmony as it may arise. The grounds for concord are many, diverse, and on balance somewhat strong—that is, their strength varies from time to time, place to place, and irrelevance to relevance for the educational task.

Let us denote some characteristic elements of the grounds for concord. The grounds are historical, yet always contemporary if the affiliation is still mutually recognized. They are an amalgam of philosophy and theology, in the sense that any real relationship depends on both the educational mission and the religious faith that joined together to establish the college and nurture its growth. The grounds are ethical and moral, for the oughtness applicable to both the institution and its members is ultimately indivisible. That is why all of this cannot be the last chapter in this exercise; we must proceed to consider not merely what church-related colleges now are (and as we have done, the skewed visions of them), but also what their true archetype is and what they have a chance to become.

But before we do proceed, let us pause long enough to employ the parenthetical pattern used above with the discussion of each source of discord as noted. What should we do (now, without using parentheses) to encourage the growth of harmony between college and church? The direction of relationships today is somewhat, and increasingly, favorable, but that does not promise the end of stress and strain. When problems appear and disputes threaten to arise, those who are identified with the colleges must remember that the critics are their own, devoted in their mind to the same heritage and the same purpose.

Sometimes the critics are angry, and if we can help it, we must not make them more so. Sometimes they are frightened, and we must seek to relieve their fears. Sometimes they don't have their facts straight, are untutored, even deplorably ignorant; and they need to be gently and firmly instructed. Sometimes they are dead wrong, and this must be pointed out to them in patience and good spirit.[18]

But that is only one side of what we of the colleges, full of our own sense of righteousness, must do. We must admit that the critics are sometimes dead right. When they call to attention the college's failure to live up to its own ideals—that is, to provide good teaching, or to be concerned about the individuals, or to stimulate the mind and the heart—then we must find the humility to welcome these strictures when they are accurate.

The stance of the college, then, when discord with its church is the mood of the moment, needs to be a combination of ameliorative stubbornness and mea culpa. Hail the harmony, to be sure, but heal the disharmony. When some church gets upset at one of its educational institutions, we of the academic world must find a way to bridge, not broaden, the rift. It will do no good just to condemn or, contrarily, to capitulate to a wrong-headed position.

The summary word for the state of the church-related colleges today is this: they and their sponsoring churches, closely or tentatively affiliated, have been for a long time and continue to be uneasy partners. Not everything is or ever will be completely smooth. Along with mutual appreciation, pretense is present on both sides—bland reassurance, high-blown rhetoric, charge followed by counter-charge. But "uneasy" is only the adjective, sometimes less, sometimes more. "Partners" is the noun.

Chapter Six

The Archetype

Church-related colleges are different from what they were in 1900, in the thirties, or even in the sixties. Of course, every college is different from what it once was; and more, the differences between the century's early years and the present have brought about considerable change for all of them. They have matured.

But the prime interest of this book is not the college itself as an institution. Rather, it is the particular matter of the college's relationship with its founding and/or sponsoring church. Time was when the ecclesiastical body was the more heavily weighted part in this partnership, but the passage of the years has produced, first, the balancing of the weight, and toward the end of the century, the assumption of larger influence by the educational institution. Church-related colleges have matured not only in general but also in the specifics of their affiliation.

As we move through the 'nineties, therefore, we find that most such institutions no longer fit the stereotypes set for them in earlier, simpler times, or still applied to them today by those who think in earlier, simpler terms. Except for the institutions on the opposite edges of the total company, the majority in the middle are doubly proud: they delight in their being "private" or "independent" or whatever description means that they can call their own educational tune, and they cherish their tie to the community of faith that founded them. The schools on the edges—we dare not say "top" and "bottom," or even "left" and "right"—are still largely dependent or, in the other direction, have finally cut the cord if not the memory. The large plurality are both free and committed.[1]

The combination of free and committed could well be the beginning of a new definition that we badly need, in order to put the old stereotypes behind us. Those outmoded notions may be summed up in two outlooks on the church-college connection: (1) the view of churchmen and secularists, arriving at a similar analysis during the twentieth century but disagreeing about its meaning (chapters 2 and 3); and (2) the view of the neoconservatives in recent decades (chapter 4). As we have seen, neither opinion is accurate or helpful.

In each case, the effort at description turned, perhaps inevitably, into prescription. Certain churchmen and their somewhat gullible counterparts, certain secularists, thought their colleges fit patterns of external qualifications or requirements, and before long they thought they *should* fit them. The only difference was that the churchmen applauded, whereas the secularists deplored, the marks of identification; in any event they stuffed the colleges into the same straitjacket. As for the neoconservatives, their emphasis on orthodoxy for the campus made them prescriptive from the start, especially when they could find very few colleges that lived up to their expectations.[2]

In the meantime, the church-related colleges themselves were not so much defining as developing. That is, theirs was not so much a corporate effort at self-description as it was simply a normal, ebb-and-flow, maturing process. To be sure, all through the century when they would get together in denominational groups or in Protestant, Catholic, and interfaith conclaves, they would talk about what "church-related" meant and should mean, and about less or more restrictive terms, "religious," "Christian," "evangelical." They talked so much they often got tired of it, more so perhaps than their affiliated churches seemed to do.[3]

Anyway, their having arrived at a condition at variance with what others said it ought to be did not mean that the colleges had succeeded in defining themselves. To be free and committed, to be both independent and dependent—and in wildly differing ratios from group to group, church to church—did not constitute a full-fledged credible description of a church-related institution. It was just the beginning. What *is* it that these colleges have become, or are in process of becoming? The question is not so much, What is the typical church-related college of today? That, surely, would be a dead-end inquiry, cluttered with the un- and a-typical. Rather, the question is, What is the archetype?

What Is a College?

A church-related college is, first of all, a college.

Not first in time. Many a denominational effort, keyed to the need of the locale in which it was set down, was a modest, lower-level school, and its educational level was raised as its locale grew. Before 1900, most of them were not born colleges in any strict sense; they began to be colleges after having been grade schools and high schools. Even into the twentieth century, many that had risen to genuine collegiate rank still had a pre-school division for those who needed it.[4]

To say that a church-related college is first of all a college is to speak of its present character—the status at which it has arrived rather than the level or quality of schooling with which it began. A church-related college is foremost a *college*. This means that it is not properly thought of as a business school, a finishing school, or a trade school. More to the point, it is not properly a propaganda factory, either offensively, to convert the world, or defensively, to reject the world.

It is not cheap—but the reference is not to money. It is not precious—but the reference is not to some class-conscious elitism. It is not merely for those eighteen to twenty-two, for that age span is today often observed in the breach. It is not easy for those who are ill-prepared; it is not hard for those who are fully prepared and determined.

But "college" must be defined in terms of its positives more than its negatives, and of its stretching possibilities more than its humdrum actualities. Here we are on old, familiar turf. Every self-respecting college in the land affirms, usually no less than twice a year—welcoming in the fall, farewelling in the spring—the intangible dimensions of the institution. A literate passerby might wonder why we academics perform the ritual so often, why we keep repeating ourselves ad nauseam. If he were a cynic, he would note the oft-noted discrepancy between profession and performance. If she felt at home on the campus, she'd know we were trying to keep up our courage.

Many bright and perceptive people have defined the ideal college in ways beyond my capacity to do so, and I won't try simply to duplicate them.[5] But I must at least explain what I mean by the species if I aim to describe the subspecies. In my view, a church-related entity does not begin to have any clear meaning until the entity itself is identified.

The entity in mind is, of course, the four-year (usually), postsecondary (usually), educational institution that follows along after K through 12, and bestows a bachelor's degree on the successful finisher of the course. But that is not the essence of a definition; that is just the framework.

The prize for completing all the required courses is called Bachelor of Arts, but it could be Bachelor of Fine Arts, or Bachelor of Science, or some other variant. Not likely, however, that it could be Bachelor of Recreation or Bachelor of Business; after all, we're talking about a College of Liberal Arts, to which is sometimes and properly added, and Sciences.

In other words, a college is at least partly defined by the content of its curriculum. The latitude is enormous, for it attempts to cover the best that has been thought, said, and done, or at least recorded by some means, but since it can't possibly cover all the best, room is left for lots of curricular differences among the colleges. Latin and Greek? Perhaps. Non-Western insights and achievements? Of course. Voodoo religion and even voodoo economics? Maybe. " The Colosseum . . . the Louvre Museum . . . a melody from a symphony by Strauss, a Bandel bonnett, a Shakespeare sonnet . . . Mickey Mouse"? Well, not all of it; but whatever, and however much, is included, it ought to be the raceless, genderless "top."

Funny thing about a college's rigorous content: it turns out to be an emphasis more on how-to than on what. An institution is not truly a college, no matter what subjects it offers, unless it insists on understanding instead of merely memorizing. The good, strong texts (for that's what they ought to be) are no good unless they put the mind to work. That is why physical education (in which I always participated, and which I heartily applaud) cannot hold a liberal arts candle to Plato, or Hobbes and Locke, or the Bible. And the college insists, too, on being able to express it, to write it down as well as to think it through.

To sum up at this point: a college is an educational institution with a sharp set of purposes for its clientele—to inform their minds with the best that has been produced in those fields of substance significant for the world's work, to encourage the mind to understand that substance and that work, and to foster the ability to express to others much of what is learned and understood.

All of this has been said over and over again, in a thousand different ways. No surprises here. But there are some concomitants that cannot be omitted from any realistic definition, even though their mention may endanger the near-unanimity that has carried us thus far. My intention is not to be tendentious; it is simply to make plain what else I think should be included in any characterization of the liberal arts college.

We can best put our finger on what has been left out if we return to the college's course of study. Allowing wide room for various subjects, the college normally divides them into three groupings called the humanities, the social sciences, and the natural sciences, or some similar titles equally imprecise. Make it four groups if you like, by adding, say, the arts or the fine arts. Or put the arts and the humanities together if you wish. In any event, be sure to mention the humanities by name, even if it is hard to identify them precisely.

Now this is strange: the humanities are considered to be sometimes less, sometimes more, than simply a major section of the curriculum. Less, because they are supposedly a residual category, defined in considerable measure by what the other branches omit. More, because they represent not only a subject matter but also a spirit or a perspective. The humanities have, or are supposed to have, a temper, a humane disposition, that can suffuse the total course of study.

But such a spirit is not the only atmospheric component of the curriculum as a whole. The sciences, natural and social, are subjects, to be sure, but they are also a process—the scientific method—and they foster all around them an atmosphere of objectivity. The humanities and the sciences join together, therefore, in producing both knowledge for the mind and intangibles for the spirit; and it is the latter as well as the former that make up a liberal education. Is it secular? Is it sacred? Surely it is both. The college throughout should possess something of the ethos as well as the content of both the humanities and the sciences.[6]

It follows, then, that the aim of the college is not simply a duplicate of the research university's aim, but has a somewhat specialized mandate. The old tripartite purpose—discovery, transmission, and public service—needs rephrasing for the college. Relinquishing most of the first role, discovery of knowledge, to the research university, the college can concentrate on the latter two, transmission of knowledge and service to society. In the pursuit of these two tasks, the college's special concern is for the students, that they may learn, think, feel, and serve.

The last requisite for the college is no newer than all else we have considered; it simply gets little mention because it is so readily assumed. This fundamental element is autonomy. A college that sees its mission in terms of learning, understanding, and even inspiriting, needs to possess sufficient sovereignty—not complete, to be sure, in this interdependent world—to make its own decisions about how to embody its purposes in its total practice. Autonomy is of course relative; but an institution of higher education must have enough of it to control, responsibly, its own destiny. A college must be its own arbiter.

Appendix A

What Is a Church-Related College?

The last shall be first. As this effort shifts from a brief description of a college to a somewhat more detailed description of a church-related college, the point of beginning may as well be the point where the preceding paragraph ended. The generalized comment has already been made: a church-related college is, first of all, a college. It needs to be all the things noted above, including the last item, autonomous. Since there once was an almost universal lack ot autonomy, and since that lack still exists today in some groups of church colleges, this is the place to start. Both churchmen, with their old-fashioned doubts as to whether their colleges should have autonomy, and secularists, with their ill-informed doubts as to whether any such colleges already possess it, should give way to the fact that autonomy is on the rise and that this is increasingly seen as desirable.[7]

It is here that we should take note of both the awkwardness and the appropriateness of the disjointed term, "church-related." To be sure, it does not say much. Quite purposely, it says less than "church-controlled," "church-directed," or "church-owned." It tries to say more than "church-founded" or some absurdity such as "church-sympathetic." A denominational modifier is either simply a brand-name or a gauntlet. And "Christian," unless it refers to a particular church, is apt to be a battle cry, or seem so to the whitewashed inside or the unwashed outside. Better stick, then, to the descriptive that says simply that a college possesses, and owns to, some sort of relationship with a religious body, the terms of which are not automatically disclosed by the term.[8]

"Church-related," then, is the modifier, and "college" is the noun. Whenever we run into a church-related hospital or a church-related medical school—and there are plenty of the former and a few of the latter—we expect it to be a hospital or a medical school; and in that case, whatever "church-related" means it should not change the institution's basic character. The same is true, or ought to be, for the college. When and if a college proclaims some sort of religious orientation, including when it describes itself as "Christian," it does not thereby earn for itself some spurious right to be less than a college.

Once that position is clear, we are free to consider the characteristics that more closely define not the collegiate genus but the church-somehow-related species. What is a church-related college, not at its maximum, however that were to be determined, but at its minimum? What should every church-related college be in order credibly to claim the name? In a sense, we will be looking neither for the least- nor the most-common denominator; we will not be trying to name as many or as few items as we can, to admit to, or exclude from, the fold. Rather, what are the things that such an institution must be, or have, or do, to deserve the cognomen? *Every* such institution, no matter the particular ecclesiastical body to which it bears a relationship?

I suggest that there are, basically, three requisites. One, it must have a sense, an appreciation, of its past. Two, it must have an understanding of, and must practice, its essential values. And three, it must hold on to, or build, a genuine, defensible relationship with its church. Not enough? Too much? Let us see.

I. *A church-related college must possess a sense of its past, its rootage,* and must show by its life—that is, by both its professions and its practices— that it has a lively *appreciation of its history* and present character.

At first glance this may not appear to be a very demanding qualification. The fact is, however, that if any college takes that prescription with utmost seriousness, and applies each word and phrase to its own condition, the result will prove to be, I daresay, a resounding collegiate re-definition.

Not just for now but for many years, a distressing number of colleges have seemed to feel that all that is required is a high-sounding, polysyllabic pronouncement in the annual catalogue, an easy-to-phrase, easy-to-forget statement. The other extreme is also deplorably present on occasion: the automatic rehearsal of archaic conception and activity, in word and deed, that presumably satisfies the obeisance expected toward the current con- nection. Neither of these mindless exercises fulfills the requirement.

There is no profit, of course, in turning the rostrum over to those who glaze, exaggerate, or otherwise distort the past and its significance. A simple and honest *recognition* by the college of the tie that exists with the church— this is what is initially called for. Then will come the *reflection,* or the *follow-through* from that recognition, to shape both the content and the spirit of the college to be as consistent with its ecclesiastical rootage, as harmo- nious, as its present circumstances permit it to be.

Some elaboration of these two steps may be useful. First, *the recognition.* It must be, of course, neither a boast nor an apology, just the straightforward fact: "This college was founded years ago by the Love-God-and-Neighbor Church, which believed in education and tried to do something about it."

Rephrase that sentence with the appreciate wording, and one has the beginnings of a reliable bow to the past.

The requisite recognition, however, is more than mere acknowledgment of its roots. It can, and should, go at least so far as to express the college's *appreciation* for what the church did for it at its founding and through the years. The lily needs no gilding if lily it is, but it can be called by its correct name and pictured accordingly. The church started the college off with at least some guidelines, often firm requirements, as to both content and atmosphere; and if the college honors its past, it will want to say as much truthfully and gratefully.

Ways of doing so are legion: presidential remarks on state occasions, publications of both temporary and more permanent sort, periodic tending of alumni, public announcements, even advertising. The cautions against excess are as valid as the warnings against omission when some reference would be proper. The rules of thumb ought simply to be, What is appropriate for this occasion, this medium, this audience? and, What is true?[9]

The follow-through will demand much more of the college than simply a handsome oral or written recognition. Here it is that one must put up or shut up. If an educational institution takes the public position that its founding and nurture by a religious institution were instrumental and invaluable in bringing it to its present academic condition, then it is duty bound to show how it feels not by profession alone but by performance. The college that cherishes its church relationship must give thought in its planning and space in its programs to those activities that will reflect the relationship.

Here as elsewhere it is advisable, even urgent, to guard against implying both too much and too little. I am not saying that the college should give way to the church's desires as to what the curriculum should offer or the campus provide. The safe stance, of course, is to be willing to listen to its church, but not to allow the church to prescribe. The college should not insert into its otherwise sound academic program some element that, though the church might favor it, would be academically unsound. Again, the wise strategy would be for the college to give sympathetic ear to what the church thinks, and then to make up its own mind.

But the college cannot in candor be said to be always right. What then? Here is where one is tempted to fall back upon some high-sounding but unworkable proposition, such as mutuality or joint responsibility. Yet the college does need to make its own decisions, and—not but, but and—the church has an important supporting role to play. Let the church play that role, of concern and judicious counsel, for among the college's various constituencies the church's word should be given special weight. If the college wants to retain a harmonious relationship, it will welcome the church's advice and consent, steadying but non-binding advice and frequent, non-grudging consent.

The church-affliated college that recognizes its rootage in more than mere words will give tangible evidence of that fact by *offering courses in religion* in the regular curriculum, *providing opportunities for worship* and other accepted forms of religious expression according to its denominational patterns, and *giving encouragement to a life of service,* as defined by the norms of its church. Since all these things require leadership and cost money, the college that is serious will employ the staff and furnish the sustenance necessary to get the job done, whether or not the church picks up the tab.

Let us look more carefully at what the job consists in. *First, for curricular offerings:* the contention here is not that there is a syllabus or a teaching process that all good little church colleges, or good big ones, ought to follow. The college itself should not be expected to require some courses, or any one course; and should not be expected not to.

As for the courses themselves, they might or might not be in one department. In fact, they might or might not be courses; that is, subject matter for religion might be properly placed in all sorts of other courses, not just those labelled "religion." Performance of the faculty might be by lecture, seminar, tutorial, or whatever else is normal behavior for the particular institution. Performance by students might be judged in any of several ways. Large latitude is desirable, but no room at all for doing nothing.

My Scottish forebears have influenced me to maintain that any right-thinking college intent on offering appropriate studies in religion would anchor its curriculum on the Bible. How can we in the West understand our world as well as our faith if we do not know the Scriptures? But any such line of argument simply shows how easy it is for any of us faithful to prescribe the particularities with which he or she is familiar, or grew up believing was the will of God. When it comes to offering courses in religion at church-related colleges, you may not make me do it your way; but more important, I cannot make you do it my way (even if I *am* right). The college, whatever its churchly tie, must provide for whatever it believes to be the preferred way to study religion seriously.

Much the same sort of thing must be said about the other two necessary provisions, *opportunities for worship and for service*. The large campus may need to give encouragement to more than one form of each—style of worship or type of social service. The small or highly homogeneous campus may manage well with only its own church's preferred practices. Whatever each institution should do about such provisions should turn on its own condition and its own peculiar circumstances. But for every college the central proposition is the same: the institution that has some kind or degree of denominational relationship must give its members a valid chance to understand and to participate in what its own denomination, and perhaps others as well, believes to be helpful exercises in worship and service.

Up to this point, nothing unusually demanding has been said, even though church-related colleges that fail to live up to such modest prescriptions can indeed be found. From church to church, however, and to greater or lesser degree, it is my opinion that most colleges do a fairly good job, and some a superb job, in holding in mind their religious rootage and giving evidence of it in their programs of study, worship, and service. In spite of the critics, this is perhaps more true than ever before.[10]

II. *A church-related college must have an understanding of, and must practice, the essential academic values.*

Phrased in such all-encompassing yet imprecise language, this second requirement for being church-related is deceptively modest and easy of fulfillment. But we academicians, when not engaging in one-upsmanship with each other, can often go lightly on ourselves while holding outsiders to a harder standard. Whether this demand is meaty enough for our purposes of definition will depend on what is meant by "understanding" and "practice," and especially, "the essential academic values."

Obviously, the first thing that is meant is that, before a college must *do* something, it must *be* something. Before a college practices its values, it must understand them, and to understand them, it must believe them. Then the initial requirement in this series of demands is that the church-related college recognize itself as a believing community. Later on, we shall ask whether or to what extent this must also be said of tax-supported and independent institutions, but our concern now is with the necessity that colleges acknowledging some church connection must understand, believe in, and practice their professed values.

"Believing community" is another of those mushy, almost sentimental, phrases with which church-related colleges may sometimes like to describe themselves, or to have others swallow, but which ought to have some teeth. Can communities believe? You better believe it. "We hold these truths to be self-evident . . . "—and go on to list a few propositions that aren't self-evident at all; they are matters of faith, unprovable, but widely, deeply appealing to an intelligent and conscientious citizenry. So it is with colleges in everyday life as with colonies in revolt: an institution as well as an individual needs to have a philosophy, or a faith; it needs an anchorage and a point of departure for its actions. A college has got to have some underpinnings.

As colleges and universities these days sometimes seem to wonder what they are and why, this point is often made by observers of higher education. The fashion once was, at least in some rarefied quarters, to downgrade the need for faith—which itself, of course, was a philosophy of education, if nothing more than simply a negative assertion that schools are free of values, and don't need to worry or depend on the way people think or feel. But we have pretty much got over that nihilism, and now we know that education must be based on something more than "it seemed like a good idea at the time"; it must be established on some sort of persuasive premises.[11]

The question is, What are they? And, Who is to say? And, What difference do those premises make, and should they make, in the actual life of the institution? Discussions of such matters have been especially lively of late, and I've offered more than my share of opinions. Many of the most thoughtful statements of others, however, are not out of date; and a large number of those who have contributed much to this discussion are educators and scholars, not all of whose names may be generally recognized, but who ought to be given a hearing.

Among the considerable host of academic leaders who in recent years have stated the constructive position that colleges must affirm their values and must try to live up to them are the following, whose ideas have spoken persuasively to me: Derek Bok, Wayne Booth, Ernest L. Boyer, Samuel Dubois Cook, Alice Gallin, Morris Keeton, Nannerl Keohane, Douglas Knight, James Laney, Edward LeRoy Long, Charles McCoy, Neal Malicky, Benjamin Mays, Richard Morrill, William F. Quillian, Paul Reinert, SJ, Harry E. Smith, F. Thomas Trotter, and Richard Wood. Many more deserve to be in the same listing.[12]

None of these sets him/herself up to be the John Henry Newman of our time, and certainly none of them attacks much of the college enterprise as Allan Bloom and Dinesh D'Souza delight to do.[13] This considerable company and others like them, with, expectedly, considerable differences among them, go about their academic lives with the belief that the academy (though not a church, but for some of them, maybe like a church) espouses a set of propositions or commitments that undergird and invigorate the educational endeavor, so as to make it, sometimes and something like, a community of learning. In the course of this essay I do not have either enough space or wit to describe the ideas of all. But I want to note two or three, not already named, whose thoughts along with the others' have been especially helpful to me.

In a recent address Craig Dykstra, Vice President of the Lilly Endowment, uses a pungent phrase, "communities of conviction," to describe what he thinks colleges as well as churches may become: "Religious communities of long-standing tradition have the capacity to be communities of conviction." He defines what he means by the term and holds out the hope that colleges can come to be so:

> Might it be that even secular universities are not so thoroughgoingly fragmented as they might seem? Might critics of the university be limited in their vision of it, attending too restrictively to what is said about the rhetoric and practice of critical inquiry, while ignoring completely the more latent but nonetheless still powerful constellation of truly common rhetorics and practices that sustain and make such diverse critical inquiry possible? . . . Could it be the case that many colleges and universities are forming both students and faculty through such practices and rhetorics in ways more satisfying and powerful than religious communities of conviction have been able to accomplish . . . ?[14]

To Dykstra's questions my answers are Yes, Yes, and Yes. What he calls "possibilities" are indeed present and "should be entertained." But note that the "convictions" are not the same as the "rhetorics and practices"; rather, they produce them. In other words, the convictions are more basic than the words and deeds designed to serve them. And if colleges are ever to achieve the status of true communities, it will be because their convictions are firmly held, not just describable and perhaps doable. Then we must ask, What are those convictions?

Mark Schwehn, Dean of Valparaiso, take a similarly positive tack in his newly published *Exiles from Eden.* As his subtitle says, his concern is *Religion and the Academic Vocation in America,* and he means to show "that the practice of certain spiritual virtues is and has always been essential to the process of learning, even within the secular academy." He names them: " . . . the conduct of academic life still depends upon such spiritual values as humility, faith, self-sacrifice, and charity," to which he later adds a fifth, "friendship."[15]

"The conduct of academic life" is, of course, in the hands of persons. The "virtues" Schwehn applauds are not those of the academy as an institution, but are those that an academic who has a sense of "vocation" must possess in his/her personal life and work. Schwehn "does not promise a new intellectual synthesis," or "wish to deny either the facts of pluralism or the need for a profound acknowledgment of human creativity. Spiritually grounded education . . . seeks the cultivation of those virtues that make the communal quest for the truth of matters possible. . . . [T]his conception of higher learning insists both that religion needs Enlightenment and that Enlightenment needs religion."[16]

(Before commenting on Schwehn's central thesis, perhaps we should note in passing his brief reference to church-related colleges. By mentioning "The few . . . that still do take their religious affiliations seriously," he seems to have adopted one or another of the outmoded marks that were discussed in chapter 2, above. He praises those colleges "that have maintained a clear sense of their own distinctive vocations," but he thinks David Riesman was "correct" in assuming that it is the church, not the college, that must be the responsible agent. His central argument, however, does not depend on his particular view of the church-related college.)[17]

Schwehn's contentions that "for most of Western history religion and higher learning were interdependent," and that "certain spiritual virtues are indispensable to learning," are welcome reminders.[18] We in the academic world ignore or devalue either insight to our detriment. Surely humility, faith, self-sacrifice, charity, and friendship are the stuff of our getting along with each other on the campus, or anywhere else. Personal "virtues" are closer to and suggestive of the qualities that institutions ought to have, but they are not quite the same, I think, as those that the college itself needs to embrace.

It will be clear by now that I am searching for an accurate language to describe the verbal pegs on which to hang a whole cloth of institutional character. How to phrase in shorthand the essence of the college's desired self-knowledge? "Convictions"? Not bad, in the phrase Dykstra uses, "communities of conviction." But the word sounds more personal and human than impersonal and communal. Schwehn's "virtues"? Ditto; in fact, a little more so. Moreover, each word is more at home in the church than in the academy; whereas the language we seek needs to be comfortable in both.

"Qualities"? "Characteristics"? "Premises"? Commentators, myself included, have used such words from time to time to denote what colleges possess or believe, and they may have a place as at least partial synonyms for some more substantial but overworked word. But they are, in common usage, too neutral or coolly descriptive.

I have finally decided to use "values," in full knowledge both that political talk, in such a phrase as "family values," has cheapened the word, and that scholarly talk is scornful of it. Someone has said it is "freighted with misunderstanding"; of two sorts, I suppose, unintentional and quite intended. Yet the word still gets through to ordinary folks who flinch more at pretense or mealy-mouthedness than at candor or complexity.[19]

The Prime Academic Values

What are the values to which a church-related college must subscribe? What are the ideals, or customs, or maybe even habits toward which such institutions have "an affective regard"? What are the intangible objects or qualities desirable as means for functioning, or even as ends in themselves?

Not just any values. Not even all moral values. Certainly not "spiritual" values. We're talking, remember, about the colleges, church-related to be sure, but first of all, colleges as distinct from churches. Thus our question should read, What are the essential academic values, lacking which the academic task simply cannot be rightly conducted?

For example, I don't think that cleanliness is an essential academic value; or personal generosity, or hope, or Sabbath observance, or forgiveness, or love, or ancestor worship, or modesty, or even vicarious suffering. These and any number of other values more to your own taste are nearly all admirable (though differing, of course, in their relative priority). You and I, I daresay, would want them, or their human practitioners, close around us on any campus we were to tread, even if we ourselves weren't always prepared to live up to them. But they are not what I am here calling prime academic values inherent in higher education itself.

Before embarking on their identification and discussion, let us not dismiss too quickly some values that seem fit candidates for top listing, some often advanced as indispensable. Take, for example, love, the heavyweight in the previous paragraph's list. Forgetting eros, agape, and theological overtones, we have to ask, Does love as we ordinarily speak of it qualify as an academic value? I think not. Respect? Perhaps, but not as a synonym for love. Self-respect, self-confidence, even egotism? Aw, come on; anybody who knows the academy would grant that they flourish there, but they don't always manage to be admirable.

Well then, what about collegiality? Strange how it has come to be a bad word on the campus. I would like to make a case for it, but only as something desirable, not indispensable. Tolerance? Yes; but the positive qualities of intolerance must not be forgot—intolerance for bullheaded ignorance, perhaps, or for intolerance. Looks as if we're moving toward intelligence, sophistication, love of learning, as among the indispensables; and I must quickly say that I don't believe it. Pleasant traits to have around, to be sure, but not necessary, not inescapable. (How many passable college presidents, trustees, or head coaches have you known who didn't possess . . . —but it would be rude to finish that query.)

Ah, but all this does point to objectivity, doesn't it? No. Not because it isn't useful when it exists, but simply because, in a pure state, it doesn't exist. Some folks can approach, or come close to, impartiality; maybe a larger number can attain a genuine even-handedness. But objectivity? The college and its human population only make fools of themselves when they claim to possess it. Such a claim is pseudo. In action, pseudo-objectivity is hardly distinguishable from valuelessness; and that, surely, is not a constructive academic value.

Then does this force us to consider commitment? I think so. None of these proximate values—respect and self-respect, tolerance and intolerance (in proper places and proportions), objectivity, impartiality, and the rest—is to be treated lightly, much less ignored. Yet none of them is a lodestar around which the college can find its ultimate direction. Commitment, however, is of a different order; it is essential. By its very meaning it raises the question, To what? And so we return to square one.

What are the prime academic values that a church-related college (and perhaps other kinds too) must believe in? I shall name four. On other occasions I have named six, eight, or ten, but the more numerous, the more diluted. Yet expand as you like; my list, obviously, is only suggestive, and there may indeed be room for others. Contract as you like, too; but I do not believe that any college can get along without all of the following four as a minimum.

First, *truth*. Whatever else the educational enterprise is about, and under whatever auspices, this item, or attribute, or value, is *primus inter pares*. The earliest church-related establishment in our land—state-related too— back in 1636 in Massachusetts, came to feel that its motto "Veritas" said it all. And the third earliest, down the way in Connecticut in 1701, did not mean to demote "Veritas" when it added "Lux." That neither Harvard nor Yale has been able to live up to its motto without any slippage or error through the centuries is not to be wondered at. Neither has any other educational institution, anytime, anywhere. A college does not take such a motto, such a leap of faith, and thereupon fulfill it. It aims to do so, it believes in it, it adopts the value of truth as one of its cardinal convictions, and then it does the best it can.

Truth has something serious to do with knowledge—its collection, its understanding, its dissemination, the respect and observance given to it. Data of course are important, and a high reliability in the handling of data is requisite. So in the academic world we honor truth in both content and method—accuracy as far as possible in its discovery, its description, and its announcement.

All of which pushes us to recognize that truth has something serious to do not only with knowledge but even more with integrity. The search for truth and its sharing demand a level of honesty and personal probity that applies to every part of the academic activity—classroom and laboratory, on examinations and in the privacy of the scholar's study. Ought the college to have an honor system? Perhaps; it usually doesn't hurt. But honor, as has often been said, is not a system; furthermore, there is more than one way to hold it high and try to observe it.

The allegiance to truth in its various forms can never be complete, of course, for we are human beings, not gods. When we accept truth as an essential value of our academic lives, we are called to embody or perform just as much truth as we are capable of, that's all. No known lies. No conscious manipulation of facts. No cheating. Even within our fallible limits, this is still a tall order. But we in academia cannot do without it.

Second but just as indispensable is the value of *freedom*. If truth is what we seek and try to share, then the seeking and the sharing must be unfettered. The church-related college—but we're not aiming here to be exclusive; any other kind too—needs to have free investigation, free exposition of what has been found, free-wheeling debate about whether and why it was worth finding. Exposing one's position to be tested among one's peers, engaging in the testing of others' positions, exercising a healthy skepticism—this is the meat, ideally, not only of the faculty club but also of the dormitory, not only of the scholarly journal but also of the student newspaper.

But note the inadequate verb that sets us on this tack: "the college needs . . . ," I said, but "needs" is not enough. The college needs lots of things: books, plumbing, computers, errand-runners, and income. We must be sure to take the further crucial step: the college must not only have freedom, or provide freedom; it must believe in freedom. It must be committed to freedom.

This is nothing like as easy as it sounds. The thing we want, admire, mean to acquire if we can, is not a nice round nugget, a tangible entity within our grasp. Rather, it is an amorphous value, a conviction we must possess, an unproved and unprovable assumption of faith about the desirable nature of intellectual activity. This is a value with whose absence or denial a college cannot compromise.

But not everybody thinks so. In fact, most of the world doesn't think so. Freedom of and for the academy is a bit broader than "academic freedom," as that worn phrase is usually understood, but it still has an elitist sound, as if it were different from, and something more than, what might be called regular freedom; that is, the normal lack of hindrance, except in emergencies, to move around physically and geographically, and maybe also in the political, economic, social, even theological, arenas. The Constitution takes pretty good care of the freedoms of speech, press, assembly, religion, and the National Rifle Association. The freedom for education on at least its lower levels, meaning accessibility, is supposed to be present for just about everybody.

But higher education is indeed different, at least in degree, for here freedom means not merely the presence of liberty of movement and expression. Rather, and more than that, it means the hard-won, hard-kept practice of exchanging points of view, of listening as well as of speaking, both of your/my expecting a hearing and of allowing me/you to be heard. To repeat, most of the collegiate world may not believe to this extent in freedom.

I intended to illustrate by noting that dictators, fascists, and communists don't believe in it; neither do the Ku Klux Klan, the John Birch Society, or militant fundamentalists and arrogant secularists. Then I was humbled by the thought that some of us liberals don't always believe in freedom: we want everybody to agree with us, and we sometimes shape our agenda to guarantee that desirable end. We do it often enough to prompt—though no prompting is really needed—the conservatives to charge us with being "politically correct," as if they don't likewise have their own PC agenda. So the give-and-take of the game of put-downs befouls many a college scene, and "freedom weeps."[20] None of us can claim to be always loyal to full freedom on the campus, and none of us has quite won the right to finger-point at the failure of others. But all of us who are committed to the search for truth know also that freedom in its most rigorous character, however often we fail it, must be at the heart of the academic endeavor.

The third prime academic value is as obvious, indispensable, and easily betrayed as the first two. It is *justice*. No long argumentation on its behalf is necessary, I suppose; it's just that we campus types can so easily overlook it, and forget how fully we have to make, and practice, this unprovable assumption concerning the bedrock of our collegiate behavior.

But the exercise of a little imagination may help to restore our sense of dependence on this paramount value. Postulate what the college scene would be like if it were given over to some contrary construct or course of action, or if we simply succumbed to mere neutrality on the issue: promotions to the less qualified faculty, high grades to the students with influential parents, honors and awards to less deserving but more popular figures. All of us have our campus horror stories to tell, for evenhanded justice is so very difficult—no, that is not right; the word is impossible—to achieve. But the college and its responsible human community have got to try.

Higher education is inescapably full of competition: student versus student, faculty versus faculty, discipline versus discipline, one institution versus another. That being observably true, a college simply cannot be run on the notion, anything goes. The need for fair play, or for as much of it—it's now getting to be repetitious—as one can muster, is everywhere evident on the campus. Fair play might be said to be only the handmaiden to justice, to be sure, but our effort to achieve it is indicative of our commitment to its basic rootage. When, say, a church-related college quits giving its special perquisites to, say, ministers, millionaires, and males, it gives notice that it is aiming to believe in justice.

There is one more that seems to me to stand on the same high platform of conviction, peer to the three values we have already noted, and I don't know what to call it. *Relatedness* is awkward and *universality* is pompous, though each is accurate, I think, to the concept in mind. For me at least, *kinship* says it pretty well, if one can be allowed to give it two meanings or two broad references. First, it refers to the relatedness and universality of all the inanimate material of the educational enterprise—books, ideas, experiments, discoveries, means of communication. Secondly, it refers to the relatedness even to the far corners of the universe of the human beings in the academic activity—fledgling students, eminent scholars, devoted teachers, deans, trustees, and so on. Let's take a look at each kind of kinship.

We have a strange habit in academia: our institutions often belie their nature in the names they choose for identification. It does no harm, of course, as long as those names are not taken as boundaries or limitations. To pick on two church-related neighbors for illustration: neither Southern Methodist nor Texas Christian can be Universities if they limit their knowledge to the South, their service to Methodists, their sphere of reference to Texas, or their thought patterns to Christian; and they don't. By its very nature an institution, a college, or a university must eschew arbitrary limits of place and time, nation and era, race and creed. Every such establishment worthy of the name must believe in the universality of knowledge.

Every scholar is also kin to every other. No one piece of subject matter can build a wall around itself, and yes, Mr. Donne, no student is an island, no matter her thinking so or his deserving to be. The person fully engaged in an academic arena, wherever and of whatever predilection, is at least a distant cousin of every other, even a century or a world away.

But the breathtakingness of the idea need not be saccharine. I do not hold that ideas have to be compatible, or that persons in academia have to like each other. No campus has ever yet been taken for Utopia or the Kingdom of God. In this consideration of primary academic values, the contention is simply that all study and all students are related. The word for the value is nothing so grandiose as love, not even respect; the word suggested for both parts of the proposition is *kinship*. We don't manage to practice it; we don't always act as if we believe in it; but we must believe in it: we and our academic work are all kin.

Values in Action

Well, there you are: truth, freedom, justice, and kinship. To those of you who get squeamish when talk turns to values, this exercise will sound preachy. To those of you who tend to genuflect when talk turns to values, this exercise will sound sacrilegious. Some of you might want more values named, others might want less. I won't argue with anyone who wants more, for I've been in your company late at night or on Sunday. But I'll do glad battle with anyone who thinks the college can get along with fewer. No one of those values, I submit, can be spared.

At the risk of repetition let me strive to be as clear as possible. These four things we have been thinking about (and perhaps one or two others that deserve to be in their company), are values to be believed in, to be convinced of, to be committed to, to be served. They are not items or constructs of finality, objective realities proved or demonstrated beyond any shadow of doubt. They can be, and often are, agnosticized.

Yet in the very act of saying as much, we must guard against a misapprehension coming from another direction. Values are elements or items of faith, to be sure, but seeking to identify those that are essential for the academic scene is not the same as seeking to construct an ersatz religion. No such effort is under way here. I am not interested in trying to compose a college credo, supposedly to substitute for a full-fleged system of philosophical, ethical, and religious values. Much more than what has here been mentioned, of course, is necessary to sustain any individual on his or her journey of faith.

Modest as is the proposition here being advanced, it is sufficiently bold or foolhardy—take your pick—to throw into consternation and disbelief a considerable fraction of today's academic population. My claim, simply, is that some values as matters of personal and corporate commitment are implicit in the educational enterprise itself. Further, that among these values are preeminently *truth, freedom, justice,* and universality or relatedness, or perhaps best, *kinship.* And one more insistence: since they are implicit, they need to be explicit.

All along our tortuous way we have claimed to be thinking mainly about the church-related college. In this chapter we are supposed to be describing its archetype. It behooves us then to say that a church-related college must strive to put into recognizable operation the values of truth, freedom, justice, and kinship. It won't succeed, of course; it won't ever achieve the whole truth, limitless freedom, complete justice, or uncompromising kinship. The church-related college, therefore, must not pretend to have fully succeeded, or even to be on the verge of such an impossible accomplishment. But it must try.

Up to now I have managed to block out a basic complaint of many readers, but I can keep you silent no longer. You have been saying elsewhere in our conversation, and loudly of late, "There is nothing peculiarly church-fostered, nothing distinctively denominational, about any of those recommended values." I agree with you, of course. You noticed, I am sure, that I referred to them as "academic values," not just church-related ones; and said further that they are "implicit" in higher education generally, not just in colleges of one or another churchly brand.

Then let me come clean: the academic values at the heart of the church-related endeavor are the same values that are at the heart of all other types of colleges, independent, tax-supported, even profit-making if there are such. The difference is of degree, not of kind. But we must not disparage the difference in degree, for it can be immense.

The difference in degree is not so much in the values themselves as in the college's opportunity, and willingness, to serve them effectively, to be loyal to them without apology, to be obligated in stricter fashion to strive to put the values into effect. The public sees this difference most clearly, perhaps, when there has been some monstrous failure or dereliction on the part of one or another institution of advertised religious affiliation. SMU's athletic ordeal in the 'eighties set records for media attention that various guilty state institutions haven't achieved but maybe deserved, because of who it was—Southern *Methodist*.[21] Caesar's wife has no straighter line to toe than the preacher's offspring.

Think of it this way, if you will: the central academic values are everybody's business—independent, tax-supported, church-related—but they are the church-related college's *primary* business. This is so because in the background of the state school is the legislature, but in the background of the church school is the church. By virtue of its heritage, and if it is to remain true to that heritage, the church-related college can never ignore, deny, or even give short shrift to our foursome of values. It is caught.

This is not to say that the church always lives up to these and other values that it professes, nor is it to say that legislatures flout them far and wide. It is simply to say that the church, more than other agencies that also have standards they don't always fulfill, keeps reminding itself of the values it believes in, and it reminds its progeny. The church is in the business of reminding.

As for the church-related college, its being on the receiving end of the church's continuous rehearsal of values places upon it an extra dimension of unrelenting obligation to adopt those values for its own. In my view, the church—any church—cannot expect its colleges to proclaim as part of their academic mission its own credo, that is, its theological and religious affirmations. But the church—every church, almost—does believe in the academic values of truth, freedom, justice, and kinship, as being derivative from its own central faith.

To what, then, does the church-related college testify when it comprehends and fully adopts these four academic values? It says that truth has an ultimacy about it, and so does freedom, in order to pursue the truth. It says that justice and kinship are not merely advisable but fundamental, in the very nature of things. In the background, the church—any church—is urging the college to say, "These academic necessities are of God. The first two add up to the love of God; the latter two to the equally obligatory love of neighbor." All right, if that is the way the church wants to say it, let it do so; for that is the church's province and language.

And that, make no mistake about it, is the heritage the church bequeaths to the church-related college. Though it may speak in its own idiom, the college must reflect on, and reflect, that heritage. The church undergirds its colleges' necessity to believe in the primary academic values. The state qua state cannot give these values a grounding in God and God's hope for humankind, but the church can and must, because of its nature. The sturdiness and consistency of the college's allegiance to academic values are the best way for it to be convincingly church-related.

III. There is a third ingredient in the definition of the archetype. *A church-related college must have a relationship with a church,* or perhaps with more than one, *that is credible and mutually understood.* The modifying adjectives that should surround this basic proposition are crucial for its meaning and usefulness, and thus need to be carefully chosen, else we could fold back the time and undo the argument of this piece in short order.

The first two modifiers, "credible" and "mutually understood," are surely credible and mutually understood. They are used simply to suggest that the relationship as described by either church or college ought not to be preposterous on the face of it (as is sometimes the case), and ought not to mean or imply different things to the two parties, or to provoke different expectations from them (as is also sometimes the case). The relationship has to be up front, and the words used to explain it must be honest, and accurate in accepted parlance.

In the early part of this chapter, when the three major elements of a definition were first mentioned, two adjectives were used for this third requirement that we now need to look at more closely. The first was "genuine": the college "must want to hold on to, or build, a genuine . . . relationship with its church." Lack of genuineness is not quite the same as the stresses and strains referred to in chapter 5, but they may often go hand in hand. The earlier sentence implies that the college may already have the makings of a real relationship with its denomination and simply needs to "hold on to" it. A second implication is that the college must still "build" a genuine relationship. The church needs to help out too, of course; a one-sided building won't stand up. But the effort here is to emphasize the requisite role of the college.

The second adjective in that earlier sentence was "defensible": the relationship that the college should have or create with its church must be able to be defended against both its too-harsh critics and its too-easy admirers. Remember, it is not the criticism or admiration of either the college or the church that we are concerned with here; it is the criticism or admiration of the nature and form of their *relationship*. Does the relationship make sense in form and substance? No successful defense can consist of the excuse that the relationship happened to be worked out long ago and never was changed. All sorts of aberrations have been unwisely hallowed with that moth-eaten apology.

To guard against the perpetuation of indefensible means and methods of relationship, let us ask, What does make sense? The overall answer is that college and church should be in touch with each other in such fashion as to enable each to fulfill its own purpose and destiny, in the exercise of its own autonomy, and to be supportive of each other in ways that do not compromise the autonomy of either. Let the church be the church. To that robust time-honored plea should be added its proper partner, let the college be the college.[22]

What, precisely, is "defensible"? Honoring the shared past; living out the implications of that heritage in present programs, curricular and otherwise; affirming the prime academic values that the church also affirms—these we have already noted in the paragraphs above.

But some folks want more. They think they want adjectives like "visible" or "tangible" to modify the relationship of college with church. Is an organic tie of some sort, or of several sorts, desirable? Defensible? The answer in many quarters is still likely to be Yes, but in my view it comes close to being

No. To be sure, there are relatively innocent forms of legal or constitutional contact that don't really mean very much and thus don't hurt much. Examples of the innocuous:

> —a reservation that one or more college officers be from a specified church;
> —a requirement that a goodly sprinkling of that church's adherents be on the college's board;
> —a provision that technical ownership of college property be vested in some church agency:
> —an accommodation whereby students planning on entering the ministry/priesthood be given financial benefits.

Time was when many such customs were so customary as never to be challenged, but that time is now gone. The question to be asked now is, What does it matter? It must not be asked frivolously, as if the church ought not to insist on such a silly thing. Rather, it needs to be asked seriously: What difference does it really make?

In more than merely church and college connections, the "outward and visible sign," whatever it is, is a way of testifying to an "inward and spiritual bond." If the college is not discommoded or harmed by the sign, well and good. When the organic tie is felt to be useful, and does not contradict the nature of the inner bond, the college may be willing to go along.

But when the organic tie begins to be invasive of the proper sphere of the college's decision-making, then the relationship is in trouble. The invasive element becomes dangerous to the integrity of the college as an educational institution. It can happen:

> —if the church plays too heavy a role in the choice of key college personnel;
> —if the church tells the college what and what not to teach, and how, and by whom;
> —if the choosing of the college's trustees is taken over by the church;
> —if the college starts to resent or to fear the church's use of the organic tie.

Don't let the affiliation compromise the proper academic decision-making of the college.

The desirable, defensible relationship is one primarily of mind and spirit, one consisting of a mutually recognized congruence of ultimate interests. Some of the strongest ties of colleges with their churches have almost no organizational aspects, no binding functions that either must perform for the other, no absolute requirements. Such colleges are few in number, to be sure, but the number may grow as the colleges increasingly cherish both their independence and their heritage. We are here trying to imagine the archetype, not to depict the imperfect actuality. And the ideal situation, surely, is one in which the college and its church, each true to its own nature, are on the same wave length and know it.

Let us have done with lesser definitions. A church-related college is, first, a college; and when that is said, it is an institution that honors its rootage in both profession and practice, that believes deeply in the academic values of truth, freedom, justice, and kinship, and that has a relationship with its church that is credible and mutually understood.

Chapter Seven

Prognosis

What is the future of the church-related college? What are its prospects as it moves through the last years of the twentieth century and prepares for the twenty-first?

The answers to these questions strike me as being very different from answers to the old chestnut, What *is* a church-related college? To that previous question we found that any one answer depends, at least in considerable part, on who is doing the asking. Now, however, the most audible answers seem to be more alike, though they come from disparate sources. Alike, but wrong.

To illustrate and recapitulate: some old-line churchmen, convinced that their ancient blueprint for the church-related college is still sound, find the future dim for any chance of restoration. Secularists, who disparage what the churchmen want, agree with their notion of the prospects. Neoconservatives of various ilk, who desire basic change in what they see, are almost uniformly pessimistic about its taking place as they desire. The research schools, independent and tax-supported universities alike, with no set philosophical antipathy for the small colleges, often look down on the church-related covey and give them little mind. Many would maintain that the colleges with conscious church affiliation face a bleak future.

One can make a fairly convincing case that the future for all kinds of colleges is bleak. Listen to the gloom-and-doom list: too much government interference, not enough government support, trustee irresponsibility, faculty bickering and disloyalty, student ill-preparation and immaturity, alumni disaffection, curricular chaos, not enough morals, or sense of mission, or money. Though many of these charges are true in some measure, the overall impression they leave is exaggerated, often grossly so. Higher education is going to make it, and its various parts will be around for the short and the long term, serving the country faithfully and well.

Some of the strictures apply to church-related colleges, of course, as well as to other types. My guess is that most commentators, left to their sometimes limited insights, would likely assign the bleakest of the bleak outlook to them. But here is the point of our noting the pessimism that is the current fashion: if there is a difference, based on type of college, in either a dire or an upbeat prognosis for all the institutions of higher education, those in the strongest rather than the weakest position for future service to the nation may be the church-related colleges. It is they who are most likely to confound both their critics and their mourners.

Before elaborating on that conviction, I want to suggest an explanation for the anomaly that independents and even state-relateds usually get a better press or more favorable review than church-relateds do. Public stereotypes for each of the three main groups of institutions, all of them based on impressions fifteen or more years out of date, are likely to be more unfactual and unfair for the church-related than for the independent and state-supported institutions. Say "independent" and you are liable to conjure up Ivy, or Stanford, Chicago, and Rice. Say "state school" and, if the topic isn't athletic glory or guilt, you'll provoke thoughts of Minnesota, Berkeley, or Virginia. But say " church related" and your hearer, even if fairly well informed about higher education in general, may think you refer to Joe Doaks Bible College or St. Siwash or Podunk Wesleyan.

Whereas what you had in mind were institutions of both quality and conviction—such as the majority listed in Appendices A and B. We who believe in the church-related college, not as it was once supposed to be but as it now is, have for too long allowed the assumption to go unchallenged that the truly good and faithful were very few, and were adequately represented by, even limited to, the Christian College Coalition. But this is a mistake on three counts: (1) most of the Coalition's colleges are not strong in academics; (2) most of those outside that self-anointed group are not apostate; and (3) most of the church-related colleges do strive for both excellence and faithfulness.

Confidence in the bright future of such colleges is deserved on several grounds:

> —their leadership is, on balance, better trained and more able than, say, fifty or seventy-five years ago;
> —their resources are recognized as, though still inadequate, stronger and getting more so than twenty-five years ago;

—their sense of heritage is less sentimental and more genuine than
perhaps ever before.

Their academic programs are good too, better-than-good often; and students
can get a sound education at nearly any of them. As already mentioned,
some of these colleges are rightly known for their unmistakably high
quality.

Do I hear murmurings that this catalogue of merits is on the skimpy side?
Of course it is. Those who would claim more are either starry-eyed or
hopelessly partisan. Higher education as a whole, probably deserving to be
thought of as better than it is usually considered, is today not at its highest
point of public repute. Church-related colleges, as we have already noted,
have not escaped a lower estimation.

Where Confidence Lies

When it comes to confidence in the future, for the church-related or any
other kind of college, the picture is mixed. But the largest reason for
confidence in any institution of higher education turns on what one has a
right to expect of that institution's allegiance to the academic values it
espouses and tries to emulate. Whether or not the future of the church
college is bright, and perhaps brighter than its competition, depends on,
among other things, how it defines its values, attests to their source, and
puts them into palpable operation.

In the preceding chapter we noted that the archetypical college would
need to affirm the primary academic values of truth, freedom, justice, and
kinship, but that no college is going to achieve the status of archetype. Then
what is the point of stressing values, and an institution's attachment to them?
Why emphasize atmosphere more than kudos, courses, bricks and mortar,
or other neatly measurable matters?

For prestige? Pecking order? The achievement of collegiate virtue? If so,
then the values themselves are demoted from being ultimate to being merely
proximate.

There is only one compulsive reason for a college's taking its academic
values with the utmost seriousness: to instill those values in the lives of the
people who come under the college's tutelage. It is to order all the affairs
of the institution in such fashion as to enable and encourage its pupils to
begin to appropriate the college's values for their own. This applies to

students mostly but is not limited to them: a college's belief in and practice of its academic values is for the purpose of exercising an influence on their behalf upon its total campus population, and if possible, beyond its borders. We usually expect too little: that, say, the president be approximately truthful, or the pay scales for all employees be roughly just, or the athletic scholarships be mostly aboveboard. But even in an imperfect world, this is not quite enough.

To seize on the promise of their future, colleges of church affiliation need to ask, Do we influence our students on behalf of the values we believe in and espouse? Are they freer, more honest, more humane, closer to being world citizens, because they spent time on this campus? Does this college make a lasting impact on the minds and hearts of those who come its way? The future of the church-related college lies in its being able to answer Yes, resoundingly but not bombastically, to such harsh self-examination.

If the answer is No, then we ought to close up shop. I don't believe the answer is No; and Dear Reader, I don't believe you do either. But we've got to walk a thin line of careful interpretation, to be sure we take into account the relevant data and the pertinent studies, pay our respects to the history of institutional influence, and gauge its present condition.

Let us begin with history. At one time (over fifty years ago) my wife and I claimed to have read more college histories than anyone else—a miserable boast, if true—and the prevailing impression they left on us was that the colleges had made a strong impact on the lives of their students. Or at least they thought they had. That was the case for all types, but if one type led the way, it had to be the church-related institution, with usually its stricter and more numerous rules and sharper definitions of the moral character that this group meant to foster.

By mid-century doubts were being expressed about the effect of a college education. The Hazen Foundation, led by Paul J. Braisted, was a pioneer in giving encouragement to colleges to be sensitive to character development, and one of their successful devices was a program of "Hazen Associates," who were a group of carefully selected professors hither and yon, subsidized modestly to give attention to students in the maturation. Hazen asked Philip Jacob to assess not so much the influence of the Foundation as of the colleges in this delicate and poorly defined area.

The result was the publication in 1957 of Jacob's book, *Changing Values in College,* a blockbuster at the time. It was said to have shown that "the college experience had little or no effect in altering basic student perceptions"; but Jacob himself didn't fully believe that, as is revealed by his chapter 6 on "The Peculiar Potency of Some Colleges." The more extensive answer to Jacob, also commissioned by Hazen and published in 1958, was John E. Smith's *Value Convictions and Higher Education,* in which he pointed out that Jacob was unsound in thinking that "basic values remain largely constant through college."[1]

We need a new assessment (a la Jacob) and a new critique (a la Smith). The unhappy legacy of the first exchange was that the shaky assessment got a much broader circulation than the corrective critique. In any event, colleges themselves kept right on trying to make a difference in the lives and thoughts of their students, and they often succeeded. Richard L. Morrill's useful volume of 1980, *Teaching Values in College,* stated the aim in his lengthy subtitle, *Facilitating Development of Ethical, Moral and Value Awareness in Students.*

Though Morrill himself has been President of three colleges related to three different churches (Salem in North Carolina, Moravian; Centre in Kentucky, Presbyterian; and currently the University of Richmond, Southern Baptist), he does not mention church-related colleges as constituting a special case for the consideration of values. But in the "Foreword," Edward D. Eddy, then Provost at Penn State and later President of the University of Rhode Island, points out: "Indeed, President Morrill poses between the lines some perplexing questions for the church-related college that knows well what it values and fails in its own estimation if it dares to graduate a student who does not take such values to heart and practice."[2]

Eddy is right: the future is full of "perplexing questions," but the college with a church connection "knows well what it values" and seeks to pass its values on. The time has come when we ought to give credit whenever we can. The church-related institutions that take with immense seriousness the academic values on the basis of which they try to operate, which they own to having received in large part from their parent churches, and which they want to inculcate in the lives and affections of their students, are legion. Whenever one can be sure of their identity, their names should be announced. The public reads enough of collegiate malfeasance and misbehavior today; we need, instead, to hear and cherish the news that is good.

Yet the process of such identification has its pitfalls. One must be suspicious of subjective ratings, and resist as far as possible the temptation toward partisanship. Some colleges that are deserving are bound to be skipped over from lack of knowledge, some that are no longer deserving may benefit from the time-lag in knowledge, and some are not and may never have been what they claim to be. Notwithstanding and on balance, it is still worthwhile, I believe, to try to honor those that illustrate the thesis that church-related colleges in large numbers are making a valiant effort to be loyal to their values.

This is the point at which to call the reader's attention to Appendix C, where subjectivity, though I hope not partisanship, will be riding high. It is there that I will mention names of colleges that seem to me to qualify for listing, those with which I happen to have had some intimate contact or about which I have received some reliable report. It is not useful, I think, to clutter this chapter with personal impressions, but I do want to share with you in Appendix C my own observations, sound or not as you will judge.

For example, to pick only a few out of a multitude doesn't seem quite fair. It would not be right to mention only Quaker colleges merely because their powerful influence on students seems to have been better documented. Or take a well-known evangelical campus: in their objective portrayal of Wheaton (Illinois), not exactly church-related but a strong member of the Christian College Coalition, Morris Keeton and Conrad Hilberry as outsider observers give the institution large credit for the beneficent effects it exerts. But special reference to a few individual campuses unfortunately neglects others whose influence is equally worthy of notice. And an institution's own spokesman could be a mite prejudiced: many a college president does a good job of praising the influence of his or her own campus. If you want names, take a look at Appendix C.[3]

So let the conclusion be simply stated: all over the map of higher education a lot of influence-exerting and value-sharing is going on. Church-related colleges may well be in the strongest position, for though conclusive data are not available either to prove or disprove such an educated guess, indications are present to suggest that their historical and religious rootage makes them more likely to remember what they stand for, and to stand. The vagaries of fortune for any one campus discourage a sanguine prediction as to how it will fare, but for the group as a whole the prognosis can be said to be good.

This expectation that the future of church-related higher education will be bright is at variance, as we have seen, with what some old-line church-men, some uninformed secularists, and some neoconservatives think about the church colleges; but their analyses are tired, out of date, and wrong. Let us take a look, in summary, at the chief elements of the hardheaded and hopeful prognosis. It is predictable, I believe, that:

1. The skill with which church-related colleges testify to the academic values they believe in will grow and become more effective than ever before.
2. The provision of opportunities for students and others to understand and experience the values to which the colleges are committed will also grow, enhancing and suffusing the campuses.
3. Although the organic or tangible ties of college with church are likely to diminish, the mutual appreciation of college and parent church body will increase, and the contacts between them will be, for both, less defensive and more supportive.
4. There will come to be a larger identification of common cause among the various colleges and types of colleges, across nearly all lines of demarcation. Because this development has been touched on little in the preceding pages, and because it is already beginning to take place, perhaps we should pause to notice its special significance for and effect on church-related colleges.

An increase in understanding and cooperation among colleges of all types is having and will continue to have a twofold and seemingly contradictory effect on them. To speak only about the church-related institutions, this breadth of outlook will bring to pass both a sharpening and a blurring of the differences that have long seemed to distinguish them from tax-supported and even independent schools. The sharpening is more likely to take place in pronouncements, the blurring in activities. That is, they still differ enough in heritage to talk a different line, but they do many of the same things and increasingly do them together—from cataloguing books to protesting social ills to waging athletic warfare. Only those few church-related colleges whose inherited ideology makes them separatist and defensive have any cause to fear such a development. To the rest it is a boon.

One further feature of this joint sharpening and blurring of distinctions needs to be hailed as part of our peroration. The new advantage is not gained merely, or mostly, from larger contact with other types of institutions; rather, it comes from freer, easier association with one's own kind, but bearing a different brand name. What has begun to happen, and what will increasingly transpire in collegiate circles, is the close identification of purpose and the harmonious coordination of program across denominational lines. Catholics elect Protestants and Protestants elect Catholics to their respective presidencies. Presbyterians entice faculty from Methodists and vice versa. But more important, Catholics, Presbyterians, and Methodists (to name only those that have the most colleges), and all the rest that love the higher learning, have begun to treat each other as brother and sister institutions. The collegiate world is more ecumenical than the ecclesiastical world has yet become.[4]

5. All of which leads to the last element in this upbeat, realistic prognosis: we who consider ourselves supporters of the church-related colleges of the United States will grow in our appreciation of them, and others as well will also grow in their appreciation. Not all of these colleges are as good academically as they ought to be, but on balance they are good. Not all of them are as proud of their church heritage and connection as they ought to be, but in the main they are glad about it. Not all of them take with sufficient seriousness the academic values implicit in their life—truth, freedom, justice, and kinship—but on the whole they try. Look around at what we have, and what the church-related colleges have a chance to become. And be thankful.

Appendix A

Church-Related Colleges and Universities: An Alphabetical Listing

Joan Keeton Young and Merrimon Cuninggim

Information for this alphabetical listing has been supplied by the colleges and universities themselves, and/or by various denominations, ecumenical bodies, and educational agencies. There is no one authoritative source, for many variables enter into a determination as to whether, and how, an institution can be said to be related to some religious body. (For a discussion of this problem, see pages 75-77.) Only this much can be claimed: the information in this and succeeding appendices is more accurate than any other such listing that we have seen, and appeared to us to be correct as of June 1994. *Abbreviations* used in all appendices, for religious bodies and in the names of institutions, are as follows:

AABC	- American Association of Bible Colleges
ABap	- American Baptist Churches in the USA
A/G	- Assemblies of God
AME	- African Methodist Episcopal Church
AMEZ	- African Methodist Episcopal Zion Church
ARP	- Associate Reformed Presbyterian Church
"Bap"	- Baptist colleges not related to a Baptist body
BrC	- Brethren Church
BrCC	- Brethren in Christ Church
C/Br	- Church of the Brethren
C/C	- Churches of Christ
CCC	- Christian College Coalition
C/G	- Church of God
CGP	- Church of God of Prophecy
Chr	- Christ or Christian
ChrBr	- Christian Brethren (aka Plymouth Brethren)
CMA	- Christian and Missionary Alliance
CME	- Christian Methodist Episcopal Church
CNJ	- Church of the New Jerusalem
CRC	- Christian Reformed Church in North America
CSc	- Church of Christ, Scientist (aka Christian Science Church)
Cumb	- Cumberland Presbyterian Church
Disc	- Christian Church (Disciples of Christ)

ECC	- Evangelical Covenant Church
EFC	- Evangelical Free Church of America
ELCA	- Evangelical Lutheran Church in America
ELS	- Evangelical Lutheran Synod
Epis	- Episcopal Church
FMC	- Free Methodist Church
FWB	- National Association of Free Will Baptists
GBap	- General Association of General Baptists
GBC	- Fellowship of Grace Brethren Churches
LDS	- Church of Jesus Christ of Latter-day Saints (Mormons)
LMO	- Lutheran Church, Missouri Synod
"Luth"	- Lutheran colleges not related to a Lutheran body
MBC	- Mennonite Brethren Churches
MCG	- Mennonite Church, General Conference
Menn	- Mennonite Church
Mor	- Moravian Church
Mssn	- Missionary Church
Naz	- Church of the Nazarene
nond.	- nondenominational
Orth	- Greek Orthodox Archdiocese
PCA	- Presbyterian Church in America
PCUSA	- Presbyterian Church (U.S.A.)
Pent	- Pentecostal Holiness Church
RC	- Roman Catholic Church
RCA	- Reformed Church in America
RLDS	- Reorganized Church of Jesus Christ of Latter Day Saints
RPC	- Reformed Presbyterian Church of North America
SBap	- Southern Baptist Convention
SDA	- Seventh-day Adventist Church
SDB	- Seventh Day Baptist General Conference
UBC	- (Church of the) United Brethren in Christ
UCC	- United Church of Christ
UMC	- United Methodist Church
Wes	- Wesleyan Church, or Wesleyan in college title
WIEL	- Wisconsin Evangelical Lutheran Synod
Friends	- *Note*: These words, though not abbreviations, are used to refer to
Jewish	institutions related to one or more Friends (Quaker) or Jewish bodies.
+	- Junior or community college, 2-year
*	- Not accredited by regional accrediting association as of 1994.

Colleges and universities related to one (or more) religious body, or claiming a religious orientation:

Abilene Chr. Univ., TX - C/C
Academy of the New Church, PA - CNJ
Adrian Coll., MI - UMC
Agnes Scott Coll., GA - PCUSA
*Alaska Bible Coll., AK - AABC; nond.
Alaska Pacific Univ., AK - UMC
Albertson Coll., ID - PCUSA
    (form. Coll. of Idaho)
Albertus Magnus Coll., CT - RC
Albion Coll., MI - UMC
Albright Coll, PA - UMC
Alderson-Broaddus Coll., WV - ABap
Allegheny Coll., PA - UMC
Allen Univ., SC - AME
Allentown Coll., PA - RC
Alma Coll., MI - PCUSA
Alvernia Coll., PA - RC
Alverno Coll., WI - RC
Amber Univ., TX - C/C
*American Bapt. Coll., TN - SBap; AABC
American Indian Bible Coll., AZ - A/G
American Univ., DC - UMC
+Ancilla Coll., IN - RC
Anderson Coll., SC - SBap
Anderson Univ., IN - C/G; CCC
+Andrew Coll., GA - UMC
Andrews Univ., MI - SDA
Anna Maria Coll., MA - RC
*Appalachian Bible Coll., WV - AABC; nond.
+Aquinas Coll., Milton, MA - RC
+Aquinas Coll., Newton, MA - RC
Aquinas Coll., MI - RC
+Aquinas Jr. Coll., TN - RC
*Arizona Coll. of the Bible, AZ - AABC; nond.
Arkansas Bapt. Coll., AR - "Bap"
Arkansas Coll., AR - PCUSA
*Arlington Bapt. Coll., TX - "Bap"; AABC
Asbury Coll., KY - CCC; nond.

Ashland Univ., OH - BrC
Assumption Coll., MA - RC
+Assumption Coll. for Sisters, NJ - RC
Atlanta Chr. Coll., GA - C/C; AABC
Atlantic Chr. Coll., NC (see Barton Coll.)
Atlantic Union Coll., MA - SDA
Augsburg Coll., MN - ELCA
Augustana Coll., IL - ELCA
Augustana Coll., SD - ELCA
Aurora Univ., IL - C/C
Austin Coll., TX - PCUSA
Averett Coll., VA - SBap
Avila Coll., MO - RC
Azusa Pacific, CA - C/G; FMC; CCC

+Bacone Coll., OK - ABap
Baker Univ., KS - UMC
Baldwin-Wallace Coll., OH - UMC
Baltimore Hebrew Union, MD - Jewish
*Baptist Bible Coll., MO - "Bap"; AABC
Baptist Bible Coll., PA - "Bap"; AABC
Barat Coll., IL - RC
Barber-Scotia Coll., NC - PCUSA
*Barclay Coll., KS - Friends; AABC
Bard Coll., NY - Epis
Barry Univ., FL - RC
Bartlesville Wes. Coll., OK - Wes; AABC
Barton Coll., NC - Disc (form. Atlantic Chr. Coll.)
*Bay Ridge Chr. Coll., TX - C/G
Baylor Univ., TX - SBap
Beaver Coll., PA - PCUSA
Belhaven Coll., MS - PCUSA; CCC
Bellarmine Coll., KY - RC
Belmont Abbey Coll., NC - RC
Belmont Univ., TN - SBap
Beloit Coll., WI - UCC
Benedict Coll., SC - ABap
Benedictine Coll., KS - RC
Bennett Coll., NC - UMC
Berea Coll., KY - nond.
Berean Coll., MO - A/G

Berry Coll., GA - nond.
Bethany Coll., CA - A/G; AABC
Bethany Coll., KS - ELCA
Bethany Coll., WV - Disc
+Bethany Luth. Coll., MN - ELS
Bethel Coll., IN - Mssn; CCC
Bethel Coll., KS - MCG; CCC
Bethel Coll., MN - "Bap"; CCC
Bethel Coll., TN - Cumb
Bethune-Cookman Coll., FL - UMC
Biola Univ., CA - CCC; nond.
Birmingham-Southern Coll., AL - UMC
Bishop Clarkson Coll., NE - Epis
Blackburn Coll., IL - PCUSA
Bloomfield Coll., NJ - PCUSA
Blue Mountain Coll., MS - SBap
Bluefield Coll., VA - SBap
Bluffton Coll., OH - MCG; CCC
*Bob Jones Univ., SC - nond.
*Boise Bible Coll., ID - C/C; AABC
Boston Coll., MA - RC
Boston Univ., MA - UMC
Brandeis Univ., MA - Jewish
Brescia Coll., KY - RC
+Brevard Coll., NC - UMC
Brewton-Parker Coll., GA - SBap
Briar Cliff Coll., IA - RC
Bridgewater Coll., VA - C/Br
Brigham Young Univ., HI - LDS
Brigham Young Univ., UT - LDS
Bryn Mawr Coll., PA - Friends
Buena Vista Coll., IA - PCUSA
Cabrini Coll., PA - RC
Caldwell Coll., NJ - RC
California Bapt. Coll., CA - SBap; CCC
California Luth. Univ., CA - ELCA
Calumet Coll., IN - RC
*Calvary Bible Coll., MO - AABC; nond.
Calvin Coll., MI - CRC; CCC
Campbell Univ., NC - SBap; CCC
Campbellsville Coll., KY - SBap; CCC

Canisius Coll., NY - RC
Capital Univ., OH - ELCA
Cardinal Stritch Coll., WI - RC
Carleton Coll., MN - UCC
Carlow Coll., PA - RC
Carroll Coll., MT - RC
Carroll Coll., WI - PCUSA
Carson-Newman Coll., TN - SBap
Carthage Coll., WI - ELCA
+Castle Coll., NH - RC
Catawba Coll., NC - UCC
Catholic Univ., DC - RC
Cedar Crest Coll., PA - UCC
Cedarville Coll., OH - "Bap"; CCC
Centenary Coll., LA - UMC
Centenary Coll., NJ - UMC
*Central Bapt. Coll., AR - "Bap"; AABC
*Central Bible Coll., MO - A/G; AABC
*Central Chr. Coll. of the Bible, MO - C/C; AABC
Central Coll., KS - FMC
Central Meth. Coll., MO - UMC
Central Univ. of Iowa, IA - RCA
Central Wes. Coll., SC - Wes; CCC
Centre Coll., KY - PCUSA
Chaminade Univ., HI - RC
Chapman Univ., CA - Disc
Charleston Southern Univ., SC - SBap
+Chatfield Coll., OH - RC
Chestnut Hill Coll., PA - RC
+Chowan Coll., NC - SBap
Christ Coll., CA - LMO
Christendom Coll., VA - RC
Christian Brothers Univ., TN - RC
*Christian Heritage Coll., CA - nond.
Cincinnati Bible Coll. & Sem., OH - C/C; AABC
*Circleville Bible Coll., OH - AABC; nond.
Claflin Coll., SC - UMC
Clark Atlanta Univ., GA - UMC
Clarke Coll., IA - RC
*Clear Creek Bapt. Bible Coll., KY - SBap; AABC
Cleveland Coll. of Jewish Studies, OH - Jewish

+*Clinton Jr. Coll., SC - AMEZ
  Coe Coll., IA - PCUSA
  College Misericordia, PA - RC
  Colorado Chr. Univ., CO - AABC; CCC; nond.
  Columbia Bible Coll., SC - AABC
  Columbia Chr. Coll., OR - C/C
  Columbia Coll., MO - Disc
  Columbia Coll., SC - UMC
  Columbia Union Coll., MD - SDA
  Concordia Coll., AL - LMO
  Concordia Coll., MI - LMO
  Concordia Coll., Moorhead, MN - ELCA
  Concordia Coll., St. Paul, MN - LMO
  Concordia Coll., NE - LMO
  Concordia Coll., NY - LMO
  Concordia Coll., OR - LMO
  Concordia Luth. Coll., TX - LMO
  Concordia Univ., IL - LMO
  Concordia Univ., WI - LMO
  Cornell Coll., IA - UMC
  Covenant Coll., GA (P.O. in TN) - PCA; CCC
  Creighton Univ., NE - RC
  Criswell Coll., The, TX - "Bap"
  Culver-Stockton Coll., MO - Disc
  Cumberland Coll., KY - SBap

  Dakota Wes. Univ., SD - UMC
  Dallas, Univ. of, TX - RC
  Dallas Bapt. Univ., TX - SBap; CCC
*Dallas Chr. Coll., TX - C/C; AABC
  Dana Coll., NE - ELCA
  David Lipscomb Univ., TN - C/C
  Davidson Coll., NC - PCUSA
  Davis & Elkins Coll., WV - PCUSA
  Dayton, Univ. of, OH - RC
  Deaconess Coll. of Nursing, MO -UCC
  Defiance Coll., OH - UCC
  Denver, Univ. of, CO - UMC
  DePaul Univ., IL - RC
  DePauw Univ., IN - UMC
  Detroit Mercy, Univ. of, MI - RC

Dickinson Coll., PA - UMC
Dillard Univ., LA - UMC; UCC
Divine Word Coll., IA - RC
Doane Coll., NE - UCC
Dr. Martin Luther Coll., MN - WIEL
Dominican Coll. of Blauvelt, NY - RC
Dominican Coll. of San Rafael, CA - RC
+Donnelly Coll., KS - RC
Dordt Coll., IA - CRC; CCC
Drake Univ., IA - Disc
Drew Univ., NJ - UMC
Drury Coll., MO - Disc; UCC
Dubuque, Univ. of, IA - PCUSA
Duke Univ., NC - UMC
Duquesne Univ., PA - RC
D'Youville Coll., NY - RC

Earlham Coll., IN - Friends
East Coast Bible Coll., NC - C/G; AABC
East Texas Bapt. Univ., TX - SBap
*Eastern Chr. Coll., MD - C/C
Eastern Coll., PA - ABap; CCC
Eastern Mennonite Coll., VA - Menn; CCC
Eastern Nazarene Coll., MA - Naz; CCC
Eckerd Coll., FL - PCUSA
Edgewood Coll., WI - RC
Edward Waters Coll., FL - AME
Elizabethtown Coll., PA - C/Br
Elmhurst Coll., IL - UCC
Elon Coll., NC - UCC
+Emmanuel Coll., GA - Pent
Emmanuel Coll., MA - RC
*Emmaus Bible Coll., IA - ChrBr; AABC
Emory & Henry Coll., VA - UMC
Emory Univ., GA - UMC
Erskine Coll., SC - ARP; PCUSA; CCC
*Eugene Bible Coll., OR - AABC; nond.
Eureka Coll., IL - Disc
Evangel Coll., MO - A/G; CCC
Evansville, Univ. of, IN - UMC

*Faith Bapt. Bible Coll., IA - "Bap"; AABC
Fairfield Univ., CT - RC
Faulkner Univ., AL - C/C
Felician Coll., NJ - RC
Ferrum Coll., VA - UMC
Findlay, Univ. of, OH - C/G
Fisk Univ., TN - UCC
Florida Bapt. Theol. Coll., FL - SBap
*Florida Bible Coll., FL - AABC; nond.
*Florida Chr. Coll., FL - C/C; AABC
Florida Memorial Coll., FL - ABap
Florida Southern Coll., FL - UMC
Fontbonne Coll., MO - RC
Fordham Univ., NY - RC
Franciscan Univ., OH - RC
Franklin Coll., IN - ABap
Franklin & Marshall Coll., PA - UCC
*Free Will Bapt. Bible Coll., TN - FWB; AABC
Freed-Hardeman Univ., TN - C/C
Fresno Pacific Coll., CA - MBC; CCC
Friends Univ., KS - Friends
Furman Univ., SC - SBap

Gannon Univ., PA - RC
Gardner-Webb Coll., NC - SBap
Geneva Coll., PA - RPC; CCC
George Fox Coll., OR - Friends; CCC
Georgetown Coll., KY - SBap
Georgetown Univ., DC - RC
Georgian Court Coll., NJ - RC
Gettysburg Coll., PA - ELCA
*God's Bible Coll., OH - AABC; nond.
Gonzaga Univ., WA - RC
Gordon Coll., MA - CCC; nond.
Goshen Coll., IN - Menn; CCC
Grace Bible Coll., MI - CCC; nond.
Grace Coll., IN - GBC; CCC
*Grace Coll. of the Bible, NE - AABC; nond.
Graceland Coll., IA - RLDS
Grand Canyon Univ., AZ - SBap; CCC
Grand Rapids Bapt. Coll., MI - "Bap"; CCC

*Grand Rapids Sch. of the Bible, MI - AABC; nond.
  Grand View Coll., IA - ELCA
  Great Falls, Coll. of, MT - RC
*Great Lakes Bible Coll., MI - C/C; AABC
  Greensboro Coll., NC - UMC
  Greenville Coll., IL - FMC; CCC
  Grinnell Coll., IA - UCC
  Grove City Coll., PA - PCUSA
  Guilford Coll., NC - Friends
  Gustavus Adolphus Coll., MN - ELCA
  Gwynedd-Mercy Coll., PA - RC

  Hamline Univ., MN - UMC
  Hampden-Sydney Coll., VA - PCUSA
  Hannibal-LaGrange Coll., MO - SBap
  Hanover Coll., IN - PCUSA
  Hardin-Simmons Univ., TX - SBap
  Harding Univ., AR - C/C
  Hastings Coll., NE - PCUSA
  Haverford Coll., PA - Friends
  Hebrew Coll., MA - Jewish
  Hebrew Union Coll., CA - Jewish
  Hebrew Union Coll., NY - Jewish
  Hebrew Union Coll., OH - Jewish
  Heidelberg Coll., OH - UCC
  Hellenic Coll., MA - Orth
  Hendrix Coll., AR - UMC
  Heritage Coll., WA - nond.
+Hesston Coll., KS - Menn
  High Point Coll., NC - UMC
  Hillsdale Coll., MI - nond.
  Hiram Coll., OH - Disc
+Hiwassee Coll., TN - UMC
  Hobart Coll., NY - Epis
*Hobe Sound Bible Coll., FL - AABC; nond.
+Holy Cross Coll., IN - RC
  Holy Cross, Coll. of the, MA - RC
  Holy Family Coll., PA - RC
  Holy Names Coll., CA - RC
  Hood Coll., MD - UCC
  Hope Coll., MI - RCA

Houghton Coll., NY - Wes; CCC
Houston Bapt. Univ., TX - SBap
Howard Payne Univ., TX - SBap
Huntingdon Coll., AL - UMC
Huntington Coll., IN - UBC; CCC
Huston-Tillotson Coll., TX - UCC; UMC

Idaho, Coll. of, ID (see Albertson Coll.)
Illinois Benedictine Coll., IL - RC
Illinois Coll., IL - PCUSA; UCC
Illinois Wes. Univ., IL - UMC
Immaculata Coll., PA - RC
Incarnate Word Coll., TX - RC
Indiana Wes. Univ., IN - Wes; CCC
Indianapolis, Univ. of, IN - UMC
*International Bible Coll., AL - C/C; AABC
Iona Coll., NY - RC
Iowa Wes. Coll., IA - UMC

+Jacksonville Coll., TX - "Bap"
Jamestown Coll., ND - PCUSA
Jarvis Christian Coll., TX - Disc
John Brown Univ., AR - CCC; nond.
John Carroll Univ., OH - RC
*John Wesley Coll., NC - AABC; nond.
Johnson Bible Coll., TN - C/C; AABC
Johnson C. Smith Univ., NC - PCUSA
Judaism, Univ. of, CA - Jewish
Judson Coll., AL - SBap
Judson Coll., IL - ABap; CCC
Juniata Coll., PA - C/Br

Kalamazoo Coll., MI - ABap
Kansas Newman Coll., KS - RC
Kansas Wes. Univ., KS - UMC
Kendall Coll., IL - UMC
Kentucky Chr. Coll., KY - C/C; AABC
*Kentucky Mountain Bible Coll., KY - AABC; nond.
Kentucky Wes. Coll., KY - UMC
Kenyon Coll., OH - Epis
Keuka Coll., NY - ABap

King Coll., TN - PCUSA; CCC
King's Coll., NY - CCC; nond.
King's Coll., PA - RC
Knoxville Coll., TN - PCUSA

+Labouré Coll., MA - RC
 Lafayette Coll., PA - PCUSA
 LaGrange Coll., GA - UMC
 Lake Forest Coll., IL - PCUSA
 Lakeland Coll., WI - UCC
 Lambuth Univ., TN - UMC
 Lane Coll., TN - CME
 LaRoche Coll., PA - RC
 LaSalle Univ., PA - RC
+LDS Business Coll., UT - LDS
 LaVerne, Univ. of, CA - C/Br
 Lebanon Valley Coll., PA - UMC
 Lee Coll., TN - C/G; CCC
+Lees Coll., KY - PCUSA
 Lees-McRae Coll., NC - PCUSA
 Le Moyne Coll., NY - RC
 Lemoyne-Owen Coll., TN - UCC
 Lenoir-Rhyne Coll., NC - ELCA
 LeTourneau Univ., TX - CCC; nond.
 Lewis & Clark Coll., OR - PCUSA
 Lewis Univ., IL - RC
 Liberty Univ., VA - "Bap"
 Limestone Coll., SC - nond.
 Lincoln Chr. Coll., IL - C/C; AABC
 Lindenwood Coll., MO - PCUSA
 Lindsey Wilson Coll., KY - UMC
 Linfield Coll., OR - ABap
 Livingstone Coll., NC - AMEZ
 Loma Linda Univ., CA - SDA
+Lon Morris Coll., TX - UMC
 Loras Coll., IA - RC
+Louisburg Coll., NC - UMC
 Louisiana Coll., LA - SBap
 Lourdes Coll., OH - RC
 Loyola Coll., MD - RC
 Loyola Marymount Univ., CA - RC

Loyola Univ., IL - RC
Loyola Univ., LA - RC
Lubbock Chr. Univ., TX - C/C
Luther Coll., IA - ELCA
Lutheran Bible Inst., WA - "Luth"
Lycoming Coll., PA - UMC
Lynchburg Coll., VA - Disc

Macalester Coll., MN - PCUSA
MacMurray Coll., IL - UMC
Madonna Univ., MI - RC
Magnolia Bible Coll., MS - C/C; AABC
Malone Coll., OH - Friends; CCC
Manchester Coll., IN - C/Br
*Manhattan Chr. Coll., KS - C/C; AABC
Manhattan Coll., NY - RC
+Manor Jr. Coll., PA - RC
+Maria Coll., NY - RC
Marian Coll., IN - RC
Marian Coll., WI - RC
+Marian Court Jr. Coll., MA - RC
Marist Coll., NY - RC
Marquette Univ., WI - RC
Mars Hill Coll., NC - SBap
+Martin Meth. Coll., TN - UMC
Mary, Univ. of, ND - RC
Mary Baldwin Coll., VA - PCUSA
Mary Hardin-Baylor, Univ. of, TX - SBap
+Mary Holmes Coll., MS - PCUSA
Marygrove Coll., MI - RC
+Marymount Coll., CA - RC
Marymount Coll., NY - RC
Marymount Manhattan Coll., NY - RC
Marymount Univ., VA - RC
Maryville Coll., TN - PCUSA
Marywood Coll., PA - RC
Master's Coll., The, CA - CCC; nond.
+Mater Dei Coll., NY - RC
McKendree Coll., IL - UMC
McMurry Univ., TX - UMC
McPherson Coll., KS - C/Br

Mercer Univ., GA - SBap
Mercyhurst Coll., PA - RC
Meredith Coll., NC - SBap
Merrimack Coll., MA - RC
Messiah Coll., PA - BrCC; CCC
Methodist Coll., NC - UMC
*Miami Chr. Coll., FL - EFC; AABC
Michigan Chr. Coll., MI - C/C
Mid-America Bible Coll., OK - C/G; AABC
MidAmerica Naz. Coll., KS - Naz; CCC
Midland Luth. Coll., NE - ELCA
Midway Coll., KY - Disc
Miles Coll., AL - CME
Milligan Coll., TN - C/C; CCC
Millikin Univ., IL - PCUSA
Millsaps Coll., MS - UMC
*Minnesota Bible Coll., MN - C/C; AABC
Mississippi Coll., MS - SBap; CCC
Missouri Bapt. Coll., MO - SBap
Missouri Valley Coll., MO - PCUSA
Mobile Coll., AL - SBap
Molloy Coll., NY - RC
Monmouth Coll., IL - PCUSA
+Montay Coll., IL - RC
Montreat-Anderson Coll., NC - PCUSA; CCC
Moravian Coll., PA - Mor
Morningside Coll., IA - UMC
Morris Brown Coll., GA - AME
Morris Coll., SC - "Bap"
Mt. Aloysius Coll., PA - RC
Mt. Marty Coll., SD - RC
Mt. Mary Coll., WI - RC
Mt. Mercy Coll., IA - RC
Mt. Olive Coll., NC - FWB
Mt. St. Clare Coll., IA - RC
Mt. St. Joseph, Coll. of, OH - RC
Mt. St. Mary Coll., NY - RC
Mt. St. Mary's Coll., CA - RC
Mt. St. Mary's Coll., MD - RC
Mt. St. Vincent, Coll. of, NY - RC
Mt. Senario Coll., WI - RC

Mt. Union Coll., OH - UMC
Mt. Vernon Naz. Coll., OH - Naz; CCC
Muhlenberg Coll., PA - ELCA
Muskingum Coll., OH - PCUSA

+*Nazarene Bible Coll., CO - Naz; AABC
  Nazareth Coll., NY - RC
 *Nebraska Chr. Coll., NE - C/C; AABC
  Nebraska Wes. Univ., NE - UMC
  Neumann Coll., PA - RC
  New Rochelle, Coll. of, NY - RC
  Newberry Coll., SC - ELCA
  Niagara Univ., NY - RC
  North Carolina Wes. Coll., NC - UMC
  North Central Bible Coll., MN - A/G
  North Central Coll., IL - UMC
+North Greenville Coll., SC - SBap
  North Park Coll., IL - ECC; CCC
+Northeastern Chr. Jr. Coll., PA - C/C
  Northland Coll., WI - UCC
  Northwest Chr. Coll., OR - Disc; CCC
  Northwest Coll., WA - A/G; AABC; CCC
  Northwest Naz. Coll., ID - Naz; CCC
  Northwestern Coll., IA - RCA; CCC
+Northwestern Coll., MN - CCC; nond.
  Northwestern Coll., WI - WIEL
  Notre Dame Coll., NH - RC
  Notre Dame Coll., OH - RC
  Notre Dame, Coll. of, CA - RC
  Notre Dame, Coll. of, MD - RC
  Notre Dame, Univ. of, IN - RC
  Nyack Coll., NY - CMA; CCC

Oakland City Coll., IN - GBap
Oakwood Coll., AL - SDA
Occidental Coll., CA - PCUSA
Ohio Dominican Coll., OH - RC
Ohio Northern Univ., OH - UMC
Ohio Valley Coll., WV - C/C
Ohio Wes. Univ., OH - UMC
Oklahoma Bapt. Univ., OK - SBap

Oklahoma Chr. Coll., OK - C/C
Oklahoma City Univ., OK - UMC
Olivet Coll., MI - UCC
Olivet Naz. Univ., IL - Naz; CCC
Oral Roberts Univ., OK - nond.
Ottawa Univ., KS - ABap
Otterbein Coll., OH - UMC
Ouachita Bapt. Univ., AR - SBap
Our Lady of the Elms, Coll. of, MA - RC
Our Lady of Holy Cross Coll., LA - RC
Our Lady of the Lake Univ., TX - RC
+Oxford Coll. of Emory Univ., GA - UMC
Ozark Chr. Coll., MO - C/C; AABC
Ozarks, Coll. of the, MO - PCUSA
Ozarks, Univ. of the, AR - PCUSA

Pacific Chr. Coll., CA - C/C; AABC
Pacific Luth. Univ., WA - ELCA
Pacific Union Coll., CA - SDA
Pacific Univ., OR - UCC
Pacific, Univ. of the, CA - UMC
Paine Coll., GA - CME; UMC
Palm Beach Atlantic Coll., FL - SBap; CCC
Park Coll., MO - RLDS
Parks Coll., IL - RC
Paul Quinn Coll., TX - AME
+Peace Coll., NC - PCUSA
Pepperdine Univ., CA - C/C
Pfeiffer Coll., NC - UMC
Philadelphia Coll. of Bible, PA - AABC; nond.
Philander Smith Coll., AR - UMC
Phillips Univ., OK - Disc
*Piedmont Bible Coll., NC - AABC; nond.
Pikeville Coll., KY - PCUSA
*Pillsbury Bapt. Bible Coll., MN - "Bap"
+*Pinebrook Jr. Coll., PA - AABC; nond.
Point Loma Naz. Coll., CA - Naz; CCC
Portland, Univ. of, OR - RC
Presbyterian Coll., SC - PCUSA
Presentation Coll., SD - RC
Principia Coll., IL - CSc

Providence Coll., RI - RC
*Puget Sound Chr. Coll., WA - C/C; AABC
Puget Sound, Univ. of, WA - UMC
+Queen of the Holy Rosary Coll., CA - RC
Queens Coll., NC - PCUSA
Quincy Coll., IL - RC

Randolph-Macon Coll., VA - UMC
Randolph-Macon Woman's Coll., VA - UMC
Redlands, Univ. of, CA - ABap
*Reformed Bible Coll., MI - CRC; AABC
Regis Coll., MA - RC
Regis Univ., CO - RC
+Reinhardt Coll., GA - UMC
Rhodes Coll., TN - PCUSA
Richmond, Univ. of, VA - SBap
+Ricks Coll., ID - LDS
Ripon Coll., WI - UCC
Rivier Coll., NH - RC
*Roanoke Bible Coll., NC - C/C; AABC
Roanoke Coll., VA - ELCA
Roberts Wes. Coll., NY - FMC; CCC
Rockhurst Coll., MO - RC
Rocky Mtn. Coll., MT - PCUSA; UCC; UMC
Rosary Coll., IL - RC
Rosemont Coll., PA - RC
Rust Coll., MS - UMC

Sacred Heart Univ., CT - RC
St. Ambrose Univ., IA - RC
St. Andrews Pres. Coll., NC - PCUSA
St. Anselm Coll., NH - RC
+St. Augustine Coll., IL - Epis
St. Augustine's Coll., NC - Epis
St. Benedict, Coll. of, MN - RC
St. Bonaventure Univ., NY - RC
+St. Catharine Coll., KY - RC
St. Catherine, Coll. of, MN - RC
St. Edward's Univ., TX - RC
St. Elizabeth, Coll. of, NJ - RC
St. Francis Coll., IN - RC

St. Francis Coll., NY - RC
St. Francis Coll., PA - RC
St. Francis, Coll. of, IL - RC
+St. Gregory's Coll., OK - RC
St. John Fisher Coll., NY - RC
St. John's Univ., MN - RC
St. John's Univ., NY - RC
St. Joseph Coll., CT - RC
St. Joseph the Provider, Coll. of, VT - RC
St. Joseph's Coll., IN - RC
St. Joseph's Coll., ME - RC
St. Joseph's Coll., NY - RC
St. Joseph's Coll., Suffolk Campus, NY - RC
St. Joseph's Univ., PA - RC
St. Leo Coll., FL - RC
*St. Louis Chr. Coll., MO - C/C; CCC
St. Louis Univ., MO - RC
St. Martin's Coll., WA - RC
St. Mary Coll., KS - RC
St. Mary, Coll. of, NE - RC
St. Mary-Of-The-Woods Coll., IN - RC
St. Mary's Coll., CA - RC
St. Mary's Coll., IN - RC
St. Mary's Coll., MI - RC
St. Mary's Coll., MN - RC
+St. Mary's Coll., NC - Epis
St. Mary's Univ., TX - RC
St. Meinrad Coll., IN - RC
St. Michael's Coll., VT - RC
St. Norbert Coll., WI - RC
St. Olaf Coll., MN - ELCA
St. Paul Bible Coll., MN - CMA
St. Paul's Coll., VA - Epis
St. Peter's Coll., NJ - RC
St. Rose, Coll. of, NY - RC
St. Scholastica, Coll. of, MN - RC
St. Thomas Aquinas Coll., NY - RC
St. Thomas Univ., FL - RC
St. Thomas, Univ. of, MN - RC
St. Thomas, Univ. of, TX - RC
St. Vincent Coll., PA - RC

St. Xavier Coll., IL - RC
Salem Coll., NC - Mor
Salem-Teikyo Univ., WV - SDB
Salve Regina Univ., RI - RC
Samford Univ., AL - SBap
San Diego, Univ. of, CA - RC
San Francisco, Univ. of, CA - RC
*San Jose Chr. Coll., CA - C/C; AABC
Santa Clara Univ., CA - RC
Santa Fe, Coll. of, NM - RC
Schreiner Coll., TX - PCUSA
Scranton, Univ. of, PA - RC
Seattle Pacific Univ., WA - FMC; CCC
Seattle Univ., WA - RC
*Selma Univ., AL - "Bap"
Seton Hall Univ., NJ - RC
Seton Hill Coll., PA - RC
Shaw Univ., NC - ABap
+Sheldon Jackson Coll., AK - PCUSA
Shenandoah Univ., VA - UMC
+Shorter Coll., AR - AME
Shorter Coll., GA - SBap
Siena Coll., NY - RC
Siena Heights Coll., MI - RC
Silver Lake Coll., WI - RC
Simpson Coll., CA - CMA; CCC
Simpson Coll., IA - UMC
Sioux Falls Coll., SD - ABap; CCC
South, Univ. of the, TN - Epis
Southeastern Coll., FL - A/G; AABC
Southern California Coll., CA - A/G; CCC
Southern Coll. of SDA, TN - SDA
Southern Meth. Univ., TX - UMC
Southern Naz. Univ., OK - Naz; CCC
Southwest Bapt. Univ., MO - SBap
Southwestern Adventist Coll., TX - SDA
Southwestern Assemblies of God Coll., TX - A/G; AABC
Southwestern Chr. Coll., TX - C/C
*Southwestern Coll., AZ - "Bapt"; AABC
Southwestern Coll., KS - UMC
Southwestern Coll. of Chr. Ministries, OK - Pent

Southwestern Univ., TX - UMC
Spalding Univ., KY - RC
+Spartanburg Meth. Coll., SC - UMC
Spelman Coll., GA - "Bap"
Spring Arbor Coll., MI - FMC; CCC
Spring Hill Coll., AL - RC
+Springfield Coll., IL - RC
Sterling Coll., KS - PCUSA; CCC
Stetson Univ., FL - SBap
Stillman Coll., AL - PCUSA
Stonehill Coll., MA - RC
+Sue Bennett Coll., KY - UMC
+Suomi Coll., MI - ELCA
Susquehanna Univ., PA - ELCA
Swarthmore Coll., PA - Friends
Syracuse Univ., NY - UMC

Tabor Coll., KS - MBC; CCC
Talladega Coll., AL - UCC
Taylor Univ., IN - CCC; nond.
*Tennessee Temple Univ., TN - AABC; CCC; nond.
Tennessee Wes. Coll., TN - UMC
Texas Christian Univ., TX - Disc
Texas Coll., TX - CME
Texas Lutheran Coll., TX - ELCA
Texas Wesleyan Univ., TX - UMC
Thiel Coll., PA - ELCA
Thomas More Coll., KY - RC
Toccoa Falls Coll., GA - CMA; AABC
Tomlinson Coll., TN - CGP
Tougaloo Coll., MS - Disc; UCC
Touro Coll., NY - Jewish
Transylvania Univ., KY - Disc
Trevecca Naz. Coll., TN - Naz; CCC
Trinity Bible Coll., ND - A/G; AABC
Trinity Chr. Coll., IL - CRC; CCC
Trinity Coll., DC - RC
*Trinity Coll. of Florida, FL - AABC; nond.
Trinity Coll., IL - EFC; CCC
Trinity Coll., VT - RC
Trinity Univ., TX - PCUSA

+Trocaire Coll., NY - RC
+Truett McConnell Coll., GA - SBap
 Tulsa, Univ. of, OK - PCUSA
 Tusculum Coll., TN - PCUSA

 Union Coll., KY - UMC
 Union Coll., NE - SDA
 Union Univ., TN - SBap
 Upsala Coll., NJ - ELCA
 Ursinus Coll., PA - UCC
 Ursuline Coll., OH - RC

*Valley Forge Chr. Coll., PA - A/G; AABC
 Valparaiso Univ., IN - ELCA; LMO
*Vennard Coll., IA - AABC; nond.
 Villa Julie Coll., MD - RC
+Villa Maria Coll., NY - RC
 Villanova Univ., PA - RC
 Virginia Intermont Coll., VA - SBap
 Virginia Union Univ., VA - ABap
 Virginia Wes. Coll., VA - UMC
 Viterbo Coll., WI - RC
 Voorhees Coll., SC - Epis

 Wagner Coll., NY - ELCA
 Wake Forest Univ., NC - SBap
+Waldorf Coll., IA - ELCA
 Walla Walla Coll., WA - SDA
 Walsh Coll., OH - RC
 Warner Pacific Coll., OR - C/G; CCC
 Warner Southern Coll., FL - C/G; CCC
 Warren Wilson Coll., NC - PCUSA
 Wartburg Coll., IA - ELCA
*Washington Bible Coll., MD - AABC; nond.
 Wayland Bapt. Univ., TX - SBap
 Waynesburg Coll., PA - PCUSA
 Wesley Coll., DE - UMC
 Wesleyan Coll., GA - UMC
 West Virginia Wes. Coll., WV - UMC
 Western Bapt. Coll., OR - "Bap"; AABC; CCC
 Westminster Coll., MO - PCUSA

Westminster Coll., PA - PCUSA
Westminster Coll., UT - PCUSA; UCC
Westmont Coll., CA - CCC; nond.
Wheaton Coll., IL - CCC; nond.
Wheeling Jesuit Coll., WV - RC
Whittier Coll., CA - Friends
Whitworth Coll., WA - PCUSA; CCC
Wilberforce Univ., OH - AME
Wiley Coll., TX - UMC
Willamette Univ., OR - UMC
William Carey Coll., MS - SBap
William Jewell Coll., MO - ABap; SBap
William Penn Coll., IA - Friends
William Tyndale Coll., MI - AABC; nond.
William Woods Coll., MO - Disc
Williams Baptist Coll., AR - SBap
Wilmington Coll., OH - Friends
Wilson Coll., PA - PCUSA
Wingate Coll., NC - SBap
Wisconsin Luth. Coll., WI - WIEL
Wittenberg Univ., OH - ELCA
Wofford Coll., SC - UMC
+Wood Jr. Coll., MS - UMC
Wooster, Coll. of, OH - PCUSA

Xavier Univ., LA - RC
Xavier Univ., OH - RC

*Yellowstone Bapt. Coll., MT - SBap
Yeshiva Univ., NY - Jewish
York Coll., NE - C/C
+Young Harris Coll., GA - UMC

Appendix B

Church-Related Colleges and Universities: A Listing by Religious Group Relationship

Joan Keeton Young and Merrimon Cuninggim

Information for this listing of colleges and universities by denominations, and by other religious attachments or sympathies, was furnished by the institutions, the churches, and other sources. When occasionally contradictions as to status were encountered, personal judgments on omission or inclusion have been made. See the introductory statement for Appendix A, above, where also will be found a table of abbreviations used in the lists.

Omitted from this listing are
—institutions once related to some denomination, but no longer comfortable with that identification;
—a few Catholic seminaries that do give the B.A. degree en route to theological training but do not consider that they are liberal arts colleges in the usual sense;
—institutions of undoubted piety whose age, quality, or general characteristics do not suggest that they have yet arrived at collegiate status.

African Methodist Episcopal - See METHODIST

African Methodist Episcopal Zion - See METHODIST

American Baptist - See BAPTIST

Assemblies of God
   American Indian Bible Coll., AZ
   Berean Coll., MO
   Bethany Coll., CA
 *Central Bible Coll., MO
   Evangel Coll., MO
   North Central Bible Coll., MN
   Northwest Coll., WA
   Southeastern Coll., FL

Southern California Coll., CA
Southwestern A. of G. Coll., TX
Trinity Bible Coll., ND
*Valley Forge Chr. Coll., PA

Associate Reformed Presbyterian - See PRESBYTERIAN

BAPTIST

American Baptist
Alderson-Broaddus Coll., WV
+Bacone Coll., OK
Benedict Coll., SC
Eastern Coll., PA
Florida Memorial Coll., FL
Franklin Coll., IN
Judson Coll., IL
Kalamazoo Coll., MI
Keuka Coll., NY
Linfield Coll., OR
Ottawa Univ., KS
Redlands, Univ. of, CA
Shaw Univ., NC
Sioux Falls Coll., SD
Virginia Union Univ., VA
William Jewell Coll., MO (also SBap)

Free Will Baptist
*Free Will Baptist Bible Coll., TN
Mt. Olive Coll., NC

General Baptist
Oakland City Coll., IN .

Seventh Day Baptist
Salem-Teikyo Univ., WV

Southern Baptist
*American Baptist Coll., TN
Anderson Coll., SC
Averett Coll., VA

Baylor Univ., TX
Belmont Univ., TN
Blue Mountain Coll., MS
Bluefield Coll., VA
Brewton-Parker Coll., GA
California Baptist Coll., CA
Campbell Univ., NC
Campbellsville Coll., KY
Carson-Newman Coll., TN
Charleston Southern Univ., SC
+Chowan Coll., NC
*Clear Creek Bapt. Bible Coll., KY
Cumberland Coll., KY
Dallas Baptist Univ., TX
East Texas Baptist Univ., TX
Florida Bapt. Theol. Coll., FL
Furman Univ., SC
Gardner-Webb Coll., NC
Georgetown Coll., KY
Grand Canyon Univ., AZ
Hannibal-LaGrange Coll., MO
Hardin-Simmons Univ., TX
Houston Baptist Univ., TX
Howard Payne Univ., TX
Judson Coll., AL
Louisiana Coll., LA
Mars Hill Coll., NC
Mary Hardin-Baylor, Univ. of, TX
Mercer Univ., GA
Meredith Coll., NC
Mississippi Coll., MS
Missouri Baptist Coll., MO
Mobile Coll., AL
+North Greenville Coll., SC
Oklahoma Baptist Univ., OK
Ouachita Baptist Univ., AR
Palm Beach Atlantic Coll., FL
Richmond, Univ. of, VA
Samford Univ., AL
Shorter Coll., GA
Southwest Baptist Univ., MO

Stetson Univ., FL
+Truett McConnell Coll., GA
Union Univ., TN
Virginia Intermont Coll., VA
Wake Forest Univ., NC
Wayland Baptist Univ., TX
William Carey Coll., MS
William Jewell Coll., MO (also ABap)
Williams Baptist Coll., AR
Wingate Coll., NC
*Yellowstone Baptist Coll., MT

"Baptist"
Arkansas Baptist Coll., AR
*Arlington Baptist Coll., TX
*Baptist Bible Coll., MO
Baptist Bible Coll., PA
Bethel Coll., MN
Cedarville Coll., OH
*Central Baptist Coll., AR
Criswell Coll., The, TX
*Faith Baptist Bible Coll., IA
Grand Rapids Baptist Coll., MI
+Jacksonville Coll., TX
Liberty Univ., VA
Morris Coll., SC
*Pillsbury Baptist Bible Coll., MN
*Selma Univ., AL
Spelman Coll., GA
Western Baptist Coll., OR

BRETHREN

Brethren Church
Ashland Univ., OH

Brethren in Christ
Messiah Coll., PA

Christian Brethren
*Emmaus Bible Coll., IA

Appendix B

Church of the Brethren
   Bridgewater Coll., VA
   Elizabethtown Coll., PA
   Juniata Coll., PA
   LaVerne, Univ. of, CA
   Manchester Coll., IN
   McPherson Coll., KS

Grace Brethren
   Grace Coll., IN

United Brethren in Christ
   Huntington Coll., IN

———————

Christian and Missionary Alliance
   Nyack Coll., NY
   St. Paul Bible Coll., MN
   Simpson Coll., CA
   Toccoa Falls Coll., GA

Christian Church (Disciples of Christ) - See *Disciples of Christ*

Christian Methodist Episcopal - See METHODIST

Christian Reformed Church - See REFORMED

Church of Christ, Scientist
   Principia Coll., IL

Church of God
   Anderson Univ., IN
   Azusa Pacific Univ., CA (also FMC)
   *Bay Ridge Christian Coll., TX
   East Coast Bible Coll., NC
   · Findlay, Univ. of, OH
   Lee Coll., TN
   Mid-America Bible Coll., OK
   Warner Pacific Coll., OR
   Warner Southern Coll., FL

Church of God of Prophecy
   Tomlinson Coll., TN

Church of the Brethren - See BRETHREN

Church of the Nazarene
   Eastern Nazarene Coll., MA
   MidAmerica Nazarene Coll., KS
   Mt. Vernon Nazarene Coll., OH
+*Nazarene Bible Coll., CO
   Northwest Nazarene Coll., ID
   Olivet Nazarene Univ., IL
   Point Loma Nazarene Coll., CA
   Southern Nazarene Univ., OK
   Trevecca Nazarene Coll., TN

Church of the New Jerusalem
   Academy of the New Church, PA

Churches of Christ
   Abilene Christian Univ., TX
   Amber Univ., TX
   Atlanta Christian Coll., GA
   Aurora Univ., IL
   *Boise Bible Coll., ID
   *Central Chr. Coll. of the Bible, MO
   Cincinnati Bible Coll., OH
   Columbia Christian Coll., OR
   *Dallas Christian Coll., TX
   David Lipscomb Univ., TN
   *Eastern Christian Coll., MD
   Faulkner Univ., AL
   *Florida Christian Coll., FL
   Freed-Hardeman Univ., TN
   *Great Lakes Bible Coll., MI
   Harding Univ., AR
   *International Bible Coll., AL
   Johnson Bible Coll., TN
   Kentucky Christian Coll., KY
   Lincoln Christian Coll., IL
   Lubbock Christian Univ., TX
   Magnolia Bible Coll., MS

    *Manhattan Christian Coll., KS
     Michigan Chr. Coll., MI
     Milligan Coll., TN
    *Minnesota Bible Coll., MN
    *Nebraska Christian Coll., NE
   +Northeastern Chr. Jr. Coll., PA
     Ohio Valley Coll., WV
     Oklahoma Christian Coll., OK
    *Ozark Christian Coll., MO
     Pacific Christian Coll., CA
     Pepperdine Univ., CA
    *Puget Sound Chr. Coll., WA
    *Roanoke Bible Coll., NC
    *St. Louis Christian Coll., MO
    *San Jose Christian Coll., CA
     Southwestern Chr. Coll., TX
     York Coll., NE

Cumberland Presbyterian - See PRESBYTERIAN

Disciples of Christ (Christian Church)
    Barton Coll., NC (formerly Atlantic Chr. Coll.)
    Bethany Coll., WV
    Chapman Univ., CA
    Columbia Coll., MO
    Culver-Stockton Coll., MO
    Drake Univ., IA
    Drury Coll., MO (also UCC)
    Eureka Coll., IL
    Hiram Coll., OH
    Jarvis Christian Coll., TX
    Lynchburg Coll., VA
    Midway Coll., KY
    Northwest Chr. Coll., OR
    Phillips Univ., OK
    Texas Christian Univ., TX
    Tougaloo Coll., MS (also UCC)
    Transylvania Univ., KY
    William Woods Coll., MO

Episcopal Church
  Bard Coll., NY
  Bishop Clarkson Coll., NE
  Hobart Coll., NY
  Kenyon Coll., OH
+St. Augustine Coll., IL
  St. Augustine's Coll., NC
+St. Mary's Coll., NC
  St. Paul's Coll., VA
  South, Univ. of the, TN
  Voorhees Coll., SC

Evangelical Covenant Church of America
  North Park Coll., IL

Evangelical Free Church of America
  *Miami Christian Coll., FL
  Trinity Coll., IL

Evangelical Lutheran Church in America - See LUTHERAN

Evangelical Lutheran Synod - See LUTHERAN

Free Methodist - See METHODIST

Free Will Baptist - See BAPTIST

Friends
  *Barclay Coll., KS
  Bryn Mawr Coll., PA
  Earlham Coll., IN
  Friends Univ., KS
  George Fox Coll., OR
  Guilford Coll., NC
  Haverford Coll., PA
  Malone Coll., OH
  Swarthmore Coll., PA
  Whittier Coll., CA
  William Penn Coll., IA
  Wilmington Coll., OH

Appendix B

General Baptist - See BAPTIST

Greek Orthodox
   Hellenic Coll., MA

Jewish
   Baltimore Hebrew Union, MD
   Brandeis Univ., MA
   Cleveland Coll. of Jewish Studies, OH
   Hebrew Coll., MA
   Hebrew Union Coll., CA
   Hebrew Union Coll., NY
   Hebrew Union Coll., OH
   Judaism, Univ. of, CA
   Touro Coll., NY
   Yeshiva Univ., NY

LATTER-DAY SAINTS (Mormons)

Church of Jesus Christ of Latter-day Saints
   Brigham Young Univ., HI
   Brigham Young Univ., UT
+LDS Business Coll., UT
+Ricks Coll., ID

Reorganized Church of Jesus Christ of Latter Day Saints
   Graceland Coll., IA
   Park Coll., MO

LUTHERAN

Evangelical Lutheran Church in America
   Augsburg Coll., MN
   Augustana Coll., IL
   Augustana Coll., SD
   Bethany Coll., KS
   California Lutheran Univ., CA
   Capital Univ., OH
   Carthage Coll., WI
   Concordia Coll., Moorhead, MN
   Dana Coll., NE

Gettysburg Coll., PA
Grand View Coll., IA
Gustavus Adolphus Coll., MN
Lenoir-Rhyne Coll., NC
Luther Coll., IA
Midland Lutheran Coll., NE
Muhlenberg Coll., PA
Newberry Coll., SC
Pacific Lutheran Univ., WA
Roanoke Coll., VA
St. Olaf Coll., MN
+Suomi Coll., MI
Susquehanna Univ., PA
Texas Lutheran Coll., TX
Thiel Coll., PA
Upsala Coll., NJ
Valparaiso Univ., IN (also LMO)
Wagner Coll., NY
+Waldorf Coll., IA
Wartburg Coll., IA
Wittenberg Univ., OH

Evangelical Lutheran Synod
+Bethany Lutheran Coll., MN

Lutheran Church Missouri Synod
Christ Coll., CA
Concordia Coll., AL
Concordia Coll., MI
Concordia Coll., St. Paul, MN
Concordia Coll., NE
Concordia Coll., NY
Concordia Coll., OR
Concordia Lutheran Coll., TX
Concordia Univ., IL
Concordia Univ., WI
Valparaiso Univ., IN (also ELCA)

Wisconsin Evangelical Lutheran Synod
Dr. Martin Luther Coll., MN
Northwestern Coll., WI

Appendix B

Wisconsin Lutheran Coll., WI

"Lutheran"
Lutheran Bible Inst., WA

MENNONITE

Mennonite Brethren Churches
Fresno Pacific Coll., CA
Tabor Coll., KS

Mennonite Church
Eastern Mennonite Coll., VA
Goshen Coll., IN
+Hesston Coll., KS

Mennonite Church, General Conference
Bethel Coll., KS
Bluffton Coll., OH

METHODIST

African Methodist Episcopal
Allen Univ., SC
Edward Waters Coll., FL
Morris Brown Coll., GA
Paul Quinn Coll., TX
+Shorter Coll., AR
Wilberforce Univ., OH

African Methodist Episcopal Zion
*+Clinton Junior Coll., SC
Livingstone Coll., NC

Christian Methodist Episcopal
Lane Coll., TN
Miles Coll., AL
Paine Coll., GA (also UMC)
Texas Coll., TX

158

Free Methodist
    Azusa Pacific Univ., CA (also C/G)
    Central Coll., KS
    Greenville Coll., IL
    Roberts Wesleyan Coll., NY
    Seattle Pacific Univ., WA
    Spring Arbor Coll., MI

United Methodist
    Adrian Coll., MI
    Alaska Pacific Univ., AK
    Albion Coll., MI
    Albright Coll., PA
    Allegheny Coll., PA
    American Univ., DC
 +Andrew Coll., GA
    Baker Univ., KS
    Baldwin-Wallace Coll., OH
    Bennett Coll., NC
    Bethune-Cookman Coll., FL
    Birmingham-Southern Coll., AL
    Boston Univ., MA
 +Brevard Coll., NC
    Centenary Coll., LA
    Centenary Coll., NJ
    Central Methodist Coll., MO
    Claflin Coll., SC
    Clark Atlanta Univ., GA
    Columbia Coll., SC
    Cornell Coll., IA
    Dakota Wesleyan Univ., SD
    Denver, Univ. of, CO
    DePauw Univ., IN
    Dickinson Coll., PA
    Dillard Univ., LA (also UCC)
    Drew Univ., NJ
    Duke Univ., NC
    Emory & Henry Coll., VA
    Emory Univ., GA
    Evansville, Univ. of, IN
    Ferrum Coll., VA

Florida Southern Coll., FL
Greensboro Coll., NC
Hamline Univ., MN
Hendrix Coll., AR
High Point Coll., NC
+Hiwassee Coll., TN
Huntingdon Coll., AL
Huston-Tillotson Coll., TX (also UCC)
Illinois Wesleyan Univ., IL
Indianapolis, Univ. of, IN
Iowa Wesleyan Coll., IA
Kansas Wesleyan Univ., KS
Kendall Coll., IL
Kentucky Wesleyan Coll., KY
LaGrange Coll., GA
Lambuth Univ., TN
Lebanon Valley Coll., PA
Lindsey Wilson Coll., KY
+Lon Morris Coll., TX
+Louisburg Coll., NC
Lycoming Coll., PA
MacMurray Coll., IL
+Martin Methodist Coll., TN
McKendree Coll., IL
McMurry Univ., TX
Methodist Coll., NC
Millsaps Coll., MS
Morningside Coll., IA
Mt. Union Coll., OH
Nebraska Wesleyan Univ., NE
North Carolina Wesleyan Coll., NC
North Central Coll., IL
Ohio Northern Univ., OH
Ohio Wesleyan Univ., OH
Oklahoma City Univ., OK
Otterbein Coll., OH
+Oxford Coll. of Emory Univ., GA
Pacific, Univ. of the, CA
Paine Coll., GA (also CME)
Pfeiffer Coll., NC
Philander Smith Coll., AR

Puget Sound, Univ. of, WA
Randolph-Macon Coll., VA
Randolph-Macon Woman's Coll., VA
+Reinhardt Coll., GA
Rocky Mountain Coll., MT (also PCUSA; UCC)
Rust Coll., MS
Shenandoah Univ., VA
Simpson Coll., IA
Southern Methodist Univ., TX
Southwestern Coll., KS
Southwestern Univ., TX
+Spartanburg Methodist Coll., SC
+Sue Bennett Coll., KY
Syracuse Univ., NY
Tennessee Wesleyan Coll., TN
Texas Wesleyan Univ., TX
Union Coll., KY
Virginia Wesleyan Coll., VA
Wesley Coll., DE
Wesleyan Coll., GA
West Virginia Wesleyan Coll., WV
Wiley Coll., TX
Willamette Univ., OR
Wofford Coll., SC
+Wood Junior Coll., MS
+Young Harris Coll., GA

Wesleyan
Bartlesville Wesleyan Coll., OK
Central Wesleyan Coll., SC
Houghton Coll., NY
Indiana Wesleyan Univ., IN

Missionary Church
Bethel Coll., IN

Moravian Church
Moravian Coll., PA
Salem Coll., NC

Pentecostal Holiness Church
  +Emmanuel Coll., GA
    Southwestern Coll. of Chr. Ministries, OK

PRESBYTERIAN

Associate Reformed Presbyterian
    Erskine Coll., SC (also PCUSA)

Cumberland Presbyterian
    Bethel Coll., TN

Presbyterian Church in America
    Covenant Coll., GA (P.O. in TN)

Presbyterian Church (U.S.A.)
    Agnes Scott Coll., GA
    Albertson Coll., ID (formerly Coll. of Idaho)
    Alma Coll., MI
    Arkansas Coll., AR
    Austin Coll., TX
    Barber-Scotia Coll., NC
    Beaver Coll., PA
    Belhaven Coll., MS
    Blackburn Coll., IL
    Bloomfield Coll., NJ
    Buena Vista Coll., IA
    Carroll Coll., WI
    Centre Coll., KY
    Coe Coll., IA
    Davidson Coll., NC
    Davis & Elkins Coll., WV
    Dubuque, Univ. of, IA
    Eckerd Coll., FL
    Erskine Coll., SC (also ARP)
    Grove City Coll., PA
    Hampden-Sydney Coll., VA
    Hanover Coll., IN
    Hastings Coll., NE
    Illinois Coll., IL (also UCC)
    Jamestown Coll., ND

Johnson C. Smith Univ., NC
King Coll., TN
Knoxville Coll., TN
Lafayette Coll., PA
Lake Forest Coll., IL
+Lees Coll., KY
 Lees-McRae Coll., NC
 Lewis & Clark Coll., OR
 Lindenwood Coll., MO
 Macalester Coll., MN
 Mary Baldwin Coll., VA
+Mary Holmes Coll., MS
 Maryville Coll., TN
 Millikin Univ., IL
 Missouri Valley Coll., MO
 Monmouth Coll., IL
 Montreat-Anderson Coll., NC
 Muskingum Coll., OH
 Occidental Coll., CA
 Ozarks, Coll. of the, MO
 Ozarks, Univ. of the, AR
+Peace Coll., NC
 Pikeville Coll., KY
 Presbyterian Coll., SC
 Queens Coll., NC
 Rhodes Coll., TN
 Rocky Mountain Coll., MT (also UCC; UMC)
 St. Andrews Pres. Coll., NC
 Schreiner Coll., TX
+Sheldon Jackson Coll., AK
 Sterling Coll., KS
 Stillman Coll., AL
 Trinity Univ., TX
 Tulsa, Univ. of, OK
 Tusculum Coll., TN
 Warren Wilson Coll., NC
 Waynesburg Coll., PA
 Westminster Coll., MO
 Westminster Coll., PA
 Westminster Coll., UT (also UCC)
 Whitworth Coll., WA

Wilson Coll., PA
Wooster, Coll. of, OH

Reformed Presbyterian
Geneva Coll., PA

REFORMED

Christian Reformed Church in North America
Calvin Coll., MI
Dordt Coll., IA
*Reformed Bible Coll., MI
Trinity Christian Coll., IL

Reformed Church in America
Central Univ. of Iowa, IA
Hope Coll., MI
Northwestern Coll., IA

Reorganized Church of Jesus Christ of Latter Day Saints - See LATTER-DAY SAINTS

Roman Catholic
Albertus Magnus Coll., CT
Allentown Coll., PA
Alvernia Coll., PA
Alverno Coll., WI
+Ancilla Coll., IN
Anna Maria Coll., MA
+Aquinas Coll., Milton, MA
+Aquinas Coll., Newton, MA
Aquinas Coll., MI
+Aquinas Junior Coll., TN
Assumption Coll., MA
+Assumption Coll. for Sisters, NJ
Avila Coll., MO
Barat Coll., IL
Barry Univ., FL
Bellarmine Coll., KY
Belmont Abbey Coll., NC

Benedictine Coll., KS
Boston Coll., MA
Brescia Coll., KY
Briar Cliff Coll., IA
Cabrini Coll., PA
Caldwell Coll., NJ
Calumet Coll., IN
Canisius Coll., NY
Cardinal Stritch Coll., WI
Carlow Coll., PA
Carroll Coll., MT
+Castle Coll., NH
Catholic Univ., DC
Chaminade Univ., HI
+Chatfield Coll., OH
Chestnut Hill Coll., PA
Christendom Coll., VA
Christian Brothers Univ., TN
Clarke Coll., IA
College Misericordia, PA
Creighton Univ., NE
Dallas, Univ. of, TX
Dayton, Univ. of, OH
De Paul Univ., IL
Detroit Mercy, Univ. of, MI
Divine Word Coll., IA
Dominican Coll. of Blauvelt, NY
Dominican Coll. of San Rafael, CA
+Donnelly Coll., KS
Duquesne Univ., PA
D'Youville Coll., NY
Edgewood Coll., WI
Emmanuel Coll., MA
Fairfield Univ., CT
Felician Coll., NJ
Fontbonne Coll., MO
Fordham Univ., NY
Franciscan Univ., OH
Gannon Univ., PA
Georgetown Univ., DC
Georgian Court Coll., NJ

Gonzaga Univ., WA
Great Falls, Coll. of, MT
Gwynedd-Mercy Coll., PA
+Holy Cross Coll., IN
Holy Cross, Coll. of the, MA
Holy Family Coll., PA
Holy Names Coll., CA
Illinois Benedictine Coll., IL
Immaculata Coll., PA
Incarnate Word Coll., TX
Iona Coll., NY
John Carroll Univ., OH
Kansas Newman Coll., KS
King's Coll., PA
+Labouré Coll., MA
LaRoche Coll., PA
LaSalle Univ., PA
LeMoyne Coll., NY
Lewis Univ., IL
Loras Coll., IA
Lourdes Coll., OH
Loyola Coll., MD
Loyola Marymount Univ., CA
Loyola Univ., IL
Loyola Univ., LA
Madonna Univ., MI
Manhattan Coll., NY
+Manor Junior Coll., PA
+Maria Coll., NY
Marian Coll., IN
Marian Coll., WI
+Marian Court Junior Coll., MA
Marist Coll., NY
Marquette Univ., WI
Mary, Univ. of, ND
Marygrove Coll., MI
+Marymount Coll., CA
Marymount Coll., NY
Marymount Manhattan Coll., NY
Marymount Univ., VA
Marywood Coll., PA

+Mater Dei Coll., NY
  Mercyhurst Coll., PA
  Merrimack Coll., MA
  Molloy Coll., NY
+Montay Coll., IL
  Mt. Aloysius Coll., PA
  Mt. Marty Coll., SD
  Mt. Mary Coll., WI
  Mt. Mercy Coll., IA
  Mt. St. Clare Coll., IA
  Mt. St. Joseph, Coll. of, OH
  Mt. St. Mary Coll., NY
  Mt. St. Mary's Coll., CA
  Mt. St. Mary's Coll., MD
  Mt. St. Vincent, Coll. of, NY
  Mt. Senario Coll., WI
  Nazareth Coll., NY
  Neumann Coll., PA
  New Rochelle, Coll. of, NY
  Niagara Univ., NY
  Notre Dame Coll., NH
  Notre Dame Coll., OH
  Notre Dame Coll. of, CA
  Notre Dame, Coll. of, MD
  Notre Dame, Univ. of, IN
  Ohio Dominican Coll., OH
  Our Lady of the Elms, Coll. of, MA
  Our Lady of Holy Cross Coll., LA
  Our Lady of the Lake Univ., TX
  Parks Coll., IL
  Portland, Univ. of, OR
  Presentation Coll., SD
  Providence Coll., RI
+Queen of the Holy Rosary Coll., CA
  Quincy Coll., IL
  Regis Coll., MA
  Regis Univ., CO
  Rivier Coll., NH
  Rockhurst Coll., MO
  Rosary Coll., IL
  Rosemont Coll., PA

Sacred Heart Univ., CT
St. Ambrose Univ., IA
St. Anselm Coll., NH
St. Benedict, Coll. of, MN
St. Bonaventure Univ., NY
+St. Catharine Coll., KY
St. Catherine, Coll. of, MN
St. Edward's Univ., TX
St. Elizabeth, Coll. of, NJ
St. Francis Coll., IN
St. Francis Coll., NY
St. Francis Coll., PA
St. Francis, Coll. of, IL
+St. Gregory's Coll., OK
St. John Fisher Coll., NY
St. John's Univ., MN
St. John's Univ., NY
St. Joseph Coll., CT
St. Joseph the Provider, Coll. of, VT
St. Joseph's Coll., IN
St. Joseph's Coll., ME
St. Joseph's Coll., NY
St. Joseph's Coll., Suffolk Campus, NY
St. Joseph's Univ., PA
St. Leo Coll., FL
St. Louis Univ., MO
St. Martin's Coll., WA
St. Mary Coll., KS
St. Mary, Coll. of, NE
St. Mary-of-the-Woods Coll., IN
St. Mary's Coll., CA
St. Mary's Coll., IN
St. Mary's Coll., MI
St. Mary's Coll., MN
St. Mary's Univ., TX
St. Meinrad Coll., IN
St. Michael's Coll., VT
St. Norbert Coll., WI
St. Peter's Coll., NJ
St. Rose, Coll. of, NY
St. Scholastica, Coll. of, MN

St. Thomas Aquinas Coll., NY
St. Thomas Univ., FL
St. Thomas, Univ. of, MN
St. Thomas, Univ. of, TX
St. Vincent Coll., PA
St. Xavier Coll., IL
Salve Regina Univ., RI
San Diego, Univ. of, CA
San Francisco, Univ. of, CA
Santa Clara Univ., CA
Santa Fe, Coll. of, NM
Scranton, Univ. of, PA
Seattle Univ., WA
Seton Hall Univ., NJ
Seton Hill Coll., PA
Siena Coll., NY
Siena Heights Coll., MI
Silver Lake Coll., WI
Spalding Univ., KY
Spring Hill Coll., AL
+Springfield Coll., IL
Stonehill Coll., MA
Thomas More Coll., KY
Trinity Coll., DC
Trinity Coll., VT
+Trocaire Coll., NY
Ursuline Coll., OH
Villa Julie Coll., MD
+Villa Maria Coll., NY
Villanova Univ., PA
Viterbo Coll., WI
Walsh Coll., OH
Wheeling Jesuit Coll., WV
Xavier Univ., LA
Xavier Univ., OH

Seventh-day Adventist
Andrews Univ., MI
Atlantic Union Coll., MA
Columbia Union Coll., MD
Loma Linda Univ., CA

Oakwood Coll., AL
Pacific Union Coll., CA
Southern Coll. of SDA, TN
Southwestern Adv. Coll., TX
Union Coll., NE
Walla Walla Coll., WA

Seventh Day Baptist - See BAPTIST

Southern Baptist - See BAPTIST

United Brethren in Christ - See BRETHREN

United Church of Christ
Beloit Coll., WI
Carleton Coll., MN
Catawba Coll., NC
Cedar Crest Coll., PA
Deaconess Coll. of Nursing, MO
Defiance Coll., OH
Dillard Univ., LA (also UMC)
Doane Coll., NE
Drury Coll., MO (also Disc)
Elmhurst Coll., IL
Elon Coll., NC
Fisk Univ., TN
Franklin & Marshall Coll., PA
Grinnell Coll., IA
Heidelberg Coll., OH
Hood Coll., MD
Huston-Tillotson Coll., TX (also UMC)
Illinois Coll., IL - (also PCUSA)
Lakeland Coll., WI
Lemoyne-Owen Coll., TN
Northland Coll., WI
Olivet Coll., MI
Pacific Univ., OR
Ripon Coll., WI
Rocky Mountain Coll., MT (also PCUSA; UMC)
Talladega Coll., AL
Tougaloo Coll., MS (also Disc)

Ursinus Coll., PA
Westminster Coll., UT (also PCUSA)

United Methodist - See METHODIST

Wesleyan - See METHODIST

Wisconsin Evangelical Lutheran Synod - See LUTHERAN

Nondenominational Members of the American Association of Bible Colleges (AABC)
  *Alaska Bible Coll., AK
  *Appalachian Bible Coll., WV
  *Arizona Coll. of the Bible, AZ
  *Calvary Bible Coll., MO
  *Circleville Bible Coll., OH
   Colorado Christian Univ., CO
   Columbia Bible Coll., SC
  *Eugene Bible Coll., OR
  *Florida Bible Coll., FL
  *God's Bible Coll., OH
  *Grace Coll. of the Bible, NE
+*Grand Rapids School of the Bible, MI
  *Hobe Sound Bible Coll., FL
  *John Wesley Coll., NC
  *Kentucky Mtn. Bible Coll., KY
   Philadelphia Coll. of Bible, PA
  *Piedmont Bible Coll., NC
+*Pinebrook Jr. Coll., PA
  *Southwestern Coll., AZ
  *Tennessee Temple Univ., TN
  *Trinity Coll. of Florida, FL
  *Vennard Coll., IA
  *Washington Bible Coll., MD
   William Tyndale Coll., MI

Nondenominational Members of the Christian College Coalition - (CCC)
   Asbury Coll., KY
   Biola Univ., CA

 Colorado Christian Univ., CO
 Gordon Coll., MA
 John Brown Univ., AR
 King's Coll., NY
 LeTourneau Univ., TX
 Master's Coll., The, CA
+Northwestern Coll., MN
 Taylor Univ., IN
 Westmont Coll., CA
 Wheaton Coll., IL

Nondenominational
 Berea Coll., KY
 Berry Coll, GA
*Bob Jones Univ., SC
*Christian Heritage Coll., CA
 Grace Bible Coll., MI
 Heritage Coll., WA
 Hillsdale Coll., MI
 Limestone Coll., SC
 Oral Roberts Univ., OK

Appendix C
Church-Related Colleges and Values

This appendix takes off from Dr. Edward Eddy's comment, on page 122 supra, about "the church-related college that knows well what it values" and, instead of doing nothing, tries very hard to support its values and to encourage its students to adopt them.

The text makes the point that when we know of such colleges, we should name them. But for two reasons this effort was put into an appendix. First, it is bound to be subjective, based on the limitations of one's own experience; and second, long lists of names are more appropriate in an addendum than in a text. My own experience is described in the Introduction, allowing us to proceed to the pertinent listings.

Reference to one list in chapter 7, too long for naming even here, was to the institutions that played host to the "Hazen Associates" and their value-laden efforts. The Danforth Foundation, borrowing the idea from Hazen and with its blessing, set up the "Danforth Associates" for similar purposes. During the years when W. Robert Rankin was the program's director, 1958 to 1978, faculty and their spouse associates were located in over nine hundred colleges, more than half of which were related to some church, and with over seven thousand faculty members and spouses involved. In other programs in the 'fifties and 'sixties Danforth worked with all types of colleges on matters having to do with their philosophies of education, but the Associates Program was peculiarly shaped to enhance a sense of values.

Since I had a relationship with Hazen and Danforth during each foundation's Associate days, I know something of what Hazen's contacts with scores of colleges, and Danforth's with hundreds, meant to the colleges' efforts to incorporate a sense of values into their educational programs. The full story deserves to be told, and perhaps someday will be.[1]

But to list several hundred names at this point might seem to be lacking in discrimination and up-to-dateness. We will turn, therefore, to later and derivative programs and more manageable groupings.

The 1978 volume, *Church Related Higher Education,* examined not only such education in toto, but also a small group of colleges, fourteen in number, in more depth. These schools, chosen from more than one hundred deemed fully eligible for selection, were "neither the best nor the worst" in respect to their relationship with the founding churches; but they were representative of diverse ties, creeds, and opinions, and efforts in various ways to be loyal to their several roots. The

National Council of Churches was the sponsor of the study, the Society for Values in Higher Education furnished and trained the campus visitors, and I was asked to write up the vignettes. This special group of colleges were: Austin (PCUSA), Concordia (NE; LMO), Drury (Disc and UCC), Furman (SBap), Goshen (Menn), Kalamazoo (ABap), Manchester (C/BR), Morris Brown (AME), St. Augustine's (NC; Epis), University of St. Thomas (MN; RC), Seattle University (RC), West Virginia Wesleyan (UMC), Whitworth (PCUSA), and Wittenberg (ELCA). Differing in a multitude of ways, they all respect their churches, find their values in their heritage, and seek to pass them on.[2] (See Appendix A for key to abbreviations.)

Having had a part in the study of those institutions, I am reminded of another group of church-related colleges whose efforts to live up to their professed values I have also known. As different from each other as the ones above, they have all been participants in the Board-Mentor Program of the Association of Governing Boards (AGB, the trade association of college and university trustees), or have on their own initiative undertaken the same sort of rigorous self-examination. As an outside consultant I had the chance to see how seriously they held their academic values and their religious grounding. Not all the colleges I worked with seemed to me to measure up, but those that did were: Austin and Manchester in the list above, plus Alaska Pacific (UMC), Allegheny (UMC), Baldwin-Wallace (UMC), Birmingham-Southern (UMC), Catawba (UCC), Clark Altanta (UMC), Cumberland University (TN; then Cumb.), Denver (UMC), Erskine (ARP; later also PCUSA), Hobart (Epis), Huntington (UBC), Johnson C. Smith (PCUSA), Maryville (MO; then RC), Muhlenberg (ELCA), Randolph-Macon Woman's (UMC), Rockhurst (RC), St. Louis University (RC), Southern Methodist (UMC), Stetson (SBap), Wake Forest (SBap), Warren Wilson (PCUSA), Wesleyan (GA; UMC), and Wooster (PCUSA). Other consultants in the ABG program had contacts with a variety of other church-related colleges equally worthy of being named.[3]

My church, the UMC for short, has appeared more often than any other in the listings to this point. If I were naming the colleges that seemed to me to be deficient in taking values seriously, the UMCs would sadly be present there too. It is the penalty for their having around a hundred institutions, next in number to the Roman Catholics, and for my knowing over half of them through personal contact, and my having attended umpteen times the annual tub-thumping of the Methodist Board of Higher Education.

So it seems only fair to try to identify those other United Methodist institutions that through thick and thin have managed to aim at being both good colleges and good church-related colleges. I won't be naming those that, in my opinion, have fallen short; they could turn the other cheek by putting it down to ignorance rather than to malice. Without repeating ones already in this appendix, here we go:

Albion, Bennett, Bethune-Cookman, Boston Univ., Centenary (LA), Central Methodist, Cornell (IA), Dakota Wesleyan, DePauw, Dickinson, Dillard (also

UCC), Drew, Duke, Emory, Emory & Henry, Greensboro, Hendrix, Huston-Tillotson (also UCC), Millsaps, North Central, Ohio Wesleyan, Otterbein, Paine (also CME), Pfeiffer, Philander Smith, Randolph-Macon (form. men's), Rocky Mountain (also PCUSA and UCC), Scarritt (now dec.), Simpson, Southwestern (TX), Willamette, and Wofford.[4] Sorry, equal space is not available for those colleges that feel unfairly omitted or, for that matter, included.

It *is* unfair not to mention other equally worthy schools, even if one's contacts are fewer and one's knowledge much more limited. Let me name some from what I have seen and heard—for I have done many an academic chore at non-Methodist colleges and listened to many heartwarming reports. At this late date (I mean agewise), I cannot repair my omissions; but at least I can give further instances, across a wider denominational spectrum, of institutions that are conscientious both academically and church-relatedly. And the dissatisfied reader would do us all a service if he or she not only scratched out those that ought not to be there, but also added to that list those that should be.

An eclectic company of recent formation, still adding names to the rigorous listing, is the "network" of church-related colleges drawn together in the Lilly Fellows Program in Humanities and the Arts, sponsored by Valparaiso. The Program consists not only of fellowships but also of national conferences, regional meetings, and literate publications, all addressing "two distinct but integrated" tasks: "to renew and deepen" the commitments of member institutions and the "sense of vocation" of their faculty. As of 1994, membership had grown to forty-five, including Bethune-Cookman, Concordia (NE), Goshen, and Whitworth, already mentioned, and of course, Valparaiso itself. The forty others, not much alike in many regards, but all concerned to be genuinely church-related or religiously affirmative, are: Anderson (IN; C/G), Augustana (IL; ELCA), Baylor (SBap), Berea (nond.) Boston College (RC), California Lutheran (ELCA), Calvin (CRC), Concordia Moorhead (ELCA), Creighton (RC), Davidson (PCUSA), Fairfield (RC), Fisk (UCC), Furman (SBap), Gonzaga (RC), Hope (RCA), Loyola Marymount (RC), Luther (ELCA), Marquette (RC), McPherson (C/BR), Messiah (BrCC), University of Notre Dame (RC), Pepperdine (C/C), Rivier (RC), St. Benedict (RC), St. Catherine (RC), St. John Fisher (RC), St. Mary-of-the-Woods (RC), St. Mary's (IN; RC), St. Olaf (ELCA), Samford (SBap), Seattle Pacific (FMC; CCC), University of the South (Epic), Stillman (PCUSA), Texas Wesleyan (UMC), Villanova (RC), Westminster (PA; PCUSA), Wheaton (IL; nond.), Wilberforce (AME), Xavier (LA; RC), and Xavier (OH; RC).[5]

Are there hosts of others of the same class or quality as those thus far mentioned? Of course. Do they differ from those already named and from each other in the way they feel about the church, or in the place of religion in their programs, or in the words they use to describe their convictions? Again, of course. These numerous institutions, like those named above, honor their ecclesiastical rootage and connections, believe in the academic values that should undergird their work, and strive to make a difference in the lives of their students.

As was noted in the text, some commentators who care deeply about particular forms of profession or practice find, variously, only one or two, or eight or ten, or a few score colleges that measure up. But deserving to be mentioned as genuine more-than-accredited colleges, truly church-related but not dominated, are institutions in the hundreds. I can name only those that have crossed my limited path or come into my restricted field of vision.

For example, around the mid-century (or perhaps earlier?) Phi Beta Kappa was said to be sometimes biased against church colleges, especially Catholic ones. Whether or not that impression may once have had substance to it, such a canard is now out of date. It should be noted that quite a few colleges already mentioned have chapters: Albion, Allegheny, Augustana (IL), Baylor, Birmingham-Southern, Boston College, Boston University, Cornell (IA), Davidson, Denver, DePauw, Dickinson, Drew, Duke, Emory, Fisk, Furman, Hobart, Hope, Kalamazoo, Luther, Marquette, Millsaps, Muhlenberg, Notre Dame (IN), Ohio Wesleyan, both Randolph-Macons, St. Catherine, St. Louis, St. Olaf, University of the South, Southern Methodist, Stetson, Villanova, Wake Forest, Wittenberg, Wofford, and Wooster.

Added to this congregation are others also that possess both a strong church tie and the high academic recognition of Phi Beta Kappa: Agnes Scott (PCUSA), Alma (PCUSA), Beloit (UCC), Brandeis (Jewish), Carleton (UCC), Catholic University (RC), Centre (PCUSA), Coe (PCUSA), University of Dallas (RC), Drake (Disc), Earlham (Friends), Fordham (RC), Franklin & Marshall (UCC), Georgetown (DC; RC), Gettysburg (ELCA), Grinnell (UCC), Gustavus Adolphus (ELCA), Hamline (UMC), Hampden-Sydney (PCUSA), Haverford (Friends), Hiram (Disc), Holy Cross (MA; RC), Illinois College (PCUSA and UCC), Kenyon (Epis), Lafayette (PCUSA), Lake Forest (PCUSA), Macalester (PCUSA), Manhattan (RC), Mary Baldwin (PCUSA), Occidental (PCUSA), Puget Sound (UMC), Redlands (ABap), Rhodes (PCUSA), Richmond (SBap), Ripon (UCC), Santa Clara (RC), Swarthmore (Friends), Syracuse (UMC), Texas Christian (Disc), Trinity (DC; RC), Trinity (TX; PCUSA), Tulsa (PCUSA), Ursinus (UCC), and Wilson (PCUSA). Eighty-three in all, as of 1994.[6]

But Phi Beta Kappa, of course, is no guarantor of permanent academic excellence, nor is there any such certificate for continuing religious conviction. Those who are interested in both excellence and conviction can pursue the search with the assurance that other institutions beyond the present listing may qualify. My final group for this personal testimony is of colleges not previously named that, so far as I am aware, care about both faith and learning, both academic achievement and sensitivity to values.

This final list is not long, and thus is it not prompted by an effort to be exhaustive. Rather, it is simply in response to the feeling that the following institutions ought not to be omitted. You will know others that should be in such a category. Good—the more the merrier.

First, for a score, A through G: Albertson (PCUSA), Anderson-Broaddus (ABap), Ashland (BrC), Augustana (SD; ELCA), Barat (RC), Bard (Epis), Barton (Disc), Berry (nond.), Bethany (WV; Disc), Bethel (KS; MCG), Bloomfield (PCUSA), Carroll (MT; RC), Carroll (WI; PCUSA), Culver-Stockton (Disc), David Lipscomb (C/C), DePaul (RC), Doane (UCC), Eckerd (PCUSA), Gardner-Webb (SBap), Guilford (Friends).

For another score plus one, H through O: Hood (UCC), Jamestown (PCUSA), John Carroll (RC), Juniata (C/Br), Lindenwood (PCUSA), Linfield (ABap), Loyola (MD; RC), Lynchburg (Disc), Mercer (SBap), Meredith (SBap), Miles (CME), Monmouth (IL: PCUSA), Moravian (Mor), Mt. St. Mary's (MD; RC), Muskingum (PCUSA), Newberry (ELCA), New Rochelle (RC), North Park (ECC), Northland (UCC), Oklahoma Baptist (SBap), Ottawa (ABap).

And the final score plus a few more, P through Z: Philips (Disc), Portland (RC), Presbyterian (PCUSA), Roanoke (ELCA), Rosemont (RC), St. Andrews Presbyterian (PCUSA), St. Bonaventure (RC), St. Edward's (RC), St. John's (MN; RC), St. Michael's (RC), Salem (NC; Mor), Seton Hall (RC), Spelman ("Bap"), Susquehanna (ELCA), Talladega (UCC), Transylvania (Disc), Tusculum (PCUSA), Upsala (ELCA), Villa Julie (RC), Virginia Union (ABap), Westminster (MO; PCUSA), Whittier (Friends), William Jewell (ABap and SBap), Yeshiva (Jewish).

Notes

A *List of names* to be used in the following *Notes,* to refer to books and other writings frequently cited:

ANDERSON   Richard E. Anderson. *Strategic Policy Changes at Private Colleges.* NY: Teachers College Press, 1977.

ASTIN   Alexander W. Astin and Calvin B. T. Lee. *The Invisible Colleges: A Profile of Small, Private Colleges with Limited Resources.* NY: McGraw-Hill, 1972.

BASS A   Dorothy Bass. "Ministry on the Margin: Protestants and Education." Part II, chap. 3, in HUTCHISON, q.v.

BASS B   "Revolutions, Quiet and Otherwise: Protestants and Higher Education during the 1960s," in PALMER, q.v.

BOYER   Ernest L. Boyer. *College: The Undergraduate Experience in America.* NY: Harper & Row, 1987.

BURTCHAELL   James Tunstead Burtchaell. "The Decline and Fall of the Christian College." [I], *First Things,* April 1991, and II, *First Things,* May 1991.

CONKIN   Paul K. Conkin, *Gone with the Ivy: A Biography of Vanderbilt University.* Knoxville: Univ. of Tennessee Press, 1985.

CONN   Robert H. Conn. *United Methodists and Their Colleges.* Nashville: United Methodist Board of Higher Education, 1989.

CROSSCURRENTS   *Crosscurrents.* Association for Religion and Intellectual Life. Winter 1993/94.

CUNINGGIM A   Merrimon Cuninggim. *The College Seeks Religion.* New Haven: Yale Univ. Press, 1947.

CUNINGGIM B   *The Protestant Stake in Higher Education.* Washington, D.C.: Council of Protestant Colleges and Universities, 1961.

CUNINGGIM C   "Varieties of Church-Relatedness in Higher Education." Section 1, chaps. 1, 2, 3, and 4, in PARSONAGE, q.v.

DYKSTRA   Craig Dykstra. "Communities of Conviction and the Liberal Arts." *Bulletin,* Council of Societies for the Study of Religion, September 1990.

GODARD   [James M. Godard, ed.], *The Mission of the Christian Colleqe in the Modern World.* Washington, D.C.: Council of Protestant Colleges and Universities, 1962.

GREELEY   Andrew M. Greeley. *From Backwater to Mainstream: A Profile of Catholic Higher Education.* NY: McGraw-Hill, 1969.

HAUERWAS   Stanley Hauerwas. *Christian Existence Today.* Durham, N.C.: Labyrinth Press, 1988.

HUTCHESON   Richard G. Hutcheson, Jr. "Are Church-Related Colleges Also Christian Colleges?" *Christian Century,* September 28, 1988.

HUTCHISON   William R. Hutchison, ed. *Between the Times: The Travail of the Protestant Establishment in America, 1900–1960.* Cambridge: Cambridge Univ. Press, 1989.

KEETON A   Morris Keeton. *Models and Mavericks.* NY: McGraw-Hill, 1971.

KEETON B   Morris Keeton and Conrad Hilberry. *Struggle and Promise: A Future for Colleges.* NY: McGraw-Hill, 1969.

KNIGHT   Douglas M. Knight. *Street of Dreams.* Durham, NC: Duke Univ. Press, 1989.

LONG   Edward LeRoy Long, Jr. *Higher Education as a Moral Enterprise.* Washington, D.C.: Georgetown Univ. Press, 1992.

LYNN   Robert Wood Lynn. " 'The Survival of Recognizably Protestant Colleges': Reflections on Old-Line Protestantism, 1950–1990," in MARSDEN, q.v.

MAGILL   Samuel H. Magill, ed. *The Contribution of the Church-Related College to the Public Good.* Washington, D.C.: Association of American Colleges, 1970.

MARSDEN   George M. Marsden and Bradley J. Longfield, eds. *The Secularization of the Academy.* NY: Oxford Univ. Press, 1992.

McCOY   Charles S. McCoy. *The Responsible Campus.* Nashville: United Methodist Board of Higher Education, 1972.

Notes

McINNES William McInnes. *Perspectives on the Current Status of and Emerging Policy Issues for Church-Related Colleges and Universities.* Washington, D.C.: Assn. of Governing Boards, 1991.

MORRILL Richard Morrill. *Teaching Values in College.* San Francisco: Jossey-Bass, 1980.

PACE C. Robert Pace. *Education and Evangelism: A Profile of Protestant Colleges.* NY: McGraw-Hill, 1972.

PALMER Parker J. Palmer, Barbara G. Wheeler, and James W. Fowler, eds. *Caring for the Commonweal: Education for Religious and Public Life.* Macon, Ga.: Mercer Univ. Press, 1990.

PARSONAGE Robert R. Parsonage, ed. *Church Related Higher Education.* Valley Forge: Judson Press, 1978.

PATTILLO Manning M. Pattillo, Jr., and Donald M. Mackenzie. *Church-Sponsored Higher Education in the United States.* Washington, D.C.: American Council on Education, 1966.

REINERT Paul C. Reinert, SJ. *To Turn the Tide.* Englewood Cliffs, N.J.: Prentice-Hall, 1972.

RIESMAN A David Riesman. *Constraint and Variety in American Education.* Lincoln: Univ. of Nebraska Press, 1965.

RIESMAN B Christopher Jencks and David Riesman. *The Academic Revolution.* Chicago: Univ. of Chicago Press, 1968.

RIESMAN C "The Evangelical Colleges: Untouched by the Academic Revolution." *Change*, January/February, 1981.

RINGENBERG William C. Ringenberg. *The Christian College: A History of Protestant Higher Education in America.* Grand Rapids: Christian Univ. Press, 1984.

SCHWEHN Mark R. Schwehn. *Exiles from Eden: Religion and the Academic Vocation in America*, NY: Oxford Univ. Press, 1993.

SMITH John E. Smith. *Value Convictions and Higher Education.* New Haven: Hazen Foundation, 1958.

SMYLIE James H. Smylie. "Roads to Our Present," in PARSONAGE, q.v.

TROTTER F. Thomas Trotter. *Loving God with One's Mind.* Nashville: United Methodist Board of Higher Education, 1987.

VON GRUENINGEN John Paul von Grueningen, ed. *Toward a Christian Philosophy of Higher Education.* Philadelphia: Westminster Press, 1957.

1. Three Stages of Relationship

1. For church college activity in early days, see Donald G. Tewksbury, *The Founding of American Colleges and Universities Before the Civil War* (New York: Teachers Coll., Columbia Univ., 1932), the classic treatment of its subject. Tewksbury's subtitle was, *With Particular Reference to the Religious Influence Bearing Upon the College Movement.*

See also Glenn Miller, "Protestants, Paideia, and Pioneers . . ." in PALMER: "Motives of place, prestige, and competition dominated the founding of western 'denominational' colleges" (196).

2. For late-nineteenth- and early-twentieth-century developments, see Laurence Veysey, *The Emergence of the American University* (Chicago: Univ. of Chicago Press, 1965); Charles Franklin Thwing, *A History of Higher Education in America* (NY: D. Appleton, 1906); Elbert Vaughan Wills, *The Growth of American Higher Education: Liberal, Professional and Technical* (Philadelphia: Dorrance, 1936); William Rainey Harper, *The Trend in Higher Education in America* (Chicago: Univ. of Chicago Press, 1905). For Harper's influence, see James P. Wind, *The Bible and the University: The Messianic Vision of William Rainey Harper* (Atlanta: Scholars Press, 1987). For foundations, see E. V. Hollis, *Philanthropic Foundations and Higher Education* (New York: Columbia Univ. Press, 1938).

3. Woodrow Wilson, "What is a College For?" *Scribner's,* November 1909, 576.

4. For early church-related colleges, see Tewksbury, *op.cit.*; ASTIN, chap. 2; PACE, chap. 2, "The Heritage"; RINGENBERG; SMYLIE; Albea Godbold, *The Church College of the Old South* (Durham: Duke Univ. Press, 1944); John O. Gross, *Methodist Beginnings in Higher Education* (Nashville: Methodist Board of Education, 1959). For "chapel . . . the symbol," see C. H. Patton and W. T. Field, *Eight O'Clock Chapel* (Cambridge: Houghton Mifflin, 1927), 201.

5. See CUNINGGIM A, 37-39, 42-44.

6. See Paul M. Limbert, *Denominational Policies in the Support and Supervision of Higher Education* (New York: Teachers Coll., Columbia Univ., 1929); RINGEN-BERG.

7. Biased, inadequate, or non-existent treatment of church-related colleges abounds; note, for example, R. Freeman Butts, *The College Charts Its Course* (New York: McGraw-Hill, 1939); John B. Johnston, *The Liberal College in Changing Society* (New York: Century, 1930); Frederick J. Kelly, *The American Arts College* (New York: Macmillan, 1925); Raymond A. Kent, ed., *Higher Education in America* (Boston: Ginn, 1930); Frederick Rudolph, *The American College and University* (New York: Random House, 1962).

8. See Robert Lincoln Kelly, *The American Colleges and the Social Order* (New York: Macmillan, 1940), especially chap. 21, "Relationships between the Colleges and the Churches." The recent volume by Clark Kerr and Marian Gade, *The Guardians* (Washington, D.C.: Association of Governing Boards, 1989), provides a useful discussion of boards of trustees, but under "Historical Trends" it overestimates the disaffection of church-related colleges, and interprets the proper relationship as consisting of "control" by the church, etc. (23-27).

For a lucid discussion of the legal history of church-related colleges' eligibility for some forms of state support, see Charles H. Wilson, Jr., *Tilton v. Richardson: The Search for*

Notes

Sectarianism in Education (Washington, D.C.: Association of American Colleges, 1971). In recent decades colleges have died or separated from churches for all sorts of reasons, good and bad: Western Maryland, for unnecessary fear of losing some state help for private schools; Teikyo Marycrest, for invasion by Japanese interests; Scarritt, for decline in missionary mission; Manhattanville and others, by amalgamation with neighbors; and unnamed others for irrelevance of tie, or outgrowth of church's horizons, or disapproval by the church, or lack of support.

9. See CUNINGGIM A, 219-221, 239-240, and "The Secular Atmosphere," 250-263. For the presence of religion on campus, see Robert Michaelsen, *The Study of Religion in American Universities* (New Haven: Society for Religion in Higher Education, 1965); Amos N. Wilder, ed., *Liberal Learning and Religion* (New York: Harper & Bros., 1951); Seymour A. Smith, *The American College Chaplaincy* (New York: Association Press, 1954).

10. For chapters and founding dates, see *Phi Beta Kappa, A Handbook for New Members*, 1991-1994.

For mid-century views of the church-related colleges, see Harvey Cox, *The Secular City* (New York: Macmillan, 1965), chap. 10, "The Church and the Secular University"; VON GRUENINGEN, especially chapters by Joseph Haroutunian, J. Edward Dirks, Ruth E. Eckert, and D. Elton Trueblood; GODARD, especially chapters by John Dillenberger, William H. K. Narum, and Edward D. Eddy, Jr.; MAGILL, especially Charles E. Peterson, Jr., "The Church-Related College: Whence Before Whether," 3-41, and Charles S. McCoy, "The Church-Related College in American Society," 48-64.

11. See, for example, KNIGHT, McINNES, BASS B; and William F. May, "Public Happiness and Higher Education," in PALMER.

12. See GREELEY; RIESMAN B, chap. 9, "Catholics and Their Colleges," 334-405; Joseph P. Kelly, "Secularization—Public Trust: The Development of Catholic Higher Education in the United States," in MAGILL, 70-85.

13. See Association of Catholic Colleges and Universities (ACCU), *Current Issues in Catholic Higher Education*, many volumes; note vol. 4, no. 2 (Winter 1984) and vol. 8, no. 2 (Winter 1988), especially papers by Alice Gallin (1984, 1988), Timothy Healy and John Murphy (both 1988). Both Gallin and Murphy have been executive directors of ACCU.

See also REINERT: when Reinert was President, "St. Louis University, in 1967, became the first major Catholic University to give laymen and clergy combined legal responsibility for institutional policy and operations" (111).

See also McINNES; Philip Gleason, "American Catholic Higher Education, 1940–1990," in MARSDEN, 234-258; Charles E. Curran, "Catholic Schooling: The Church and the University," in *Christian Century*, April 20, 1994, 419-421.

14. See the discussion in LYNN, 191-192, n. 2. See also HUTCHISON, especially BASS A. For numbers of colleges of each denomination, see Appendix B, below.

15. See Wade Clark Roof and William McKinney, *American Mainline Religion* (New Brunswick: Rutgers Univ. Press, 1987); Robert Wuthnow, *The Restructuring of American Religion* (Princeton: Princeton Univ. Press, 1988); HUTCHISON; BASS A.

16. See, for example, CONN: "By the mid 1980s . . . the positions of the church and college relative to one another had changed . . . [The colleges had arrived at a position of benevolent strength vis-a-vis the church . . ." (157).

182

Robert Conn's interpretation is at less variance than at first appears with that of Dorothy Bass, whose "Ministry on the Margin" seems to show the decline of the colleges; but what her essay *does* show is the decline of the churches' authority *in* their colleges, and the decline of the churches' influence *through* their colleges on higher education in general—which is an altogether sound conclusion for one writing from the church's as distinct from the college's perspective; see BASS A, 48-71.

17. Robert Wuthnow, *The Struggle for America's Soul: Evangelicals, Liberals and Secularism* (Grand Rapids: Eerdmans, 1989), especially chap. 8, "The Costs of Marginality." See also George Marsden, *Evangelicalism and Modern America* (Grand Rapids: Eerdmans, 1984).

18. See RINGENBERG, chap. 6. "Ultraconservative" is the descriptive used by HUTCHESON; see chap. 4, n. 8, below. The Christian College Coalition was established in 1976. For a description of one such institution, Covenant College, see "Christian Values and Academic Inquiry," *Chronicle of Higher Education*, November 13, 1991. The "Transnational Association of Christian Schools" that lends its approval to some "Christian" and Bible colleges has no standing among accrediting bodies; see *Chronicle of Higher Education*, September 4, 1991, and *AGB Reports*, Association of Governing Boards, October-November 1991.

See Appendix B for a listing of the member institutions of the Christian College Coalition and the American Association of Bible Colleges.

2. Admiring and Demanding Church Leaders

1. See SMYLIE; RINGENBERG; CUNINGGIM A; Paul M. Limbert, *op. cit.*; Robert L. Kelly, *op. cit.*

2. For Trinities, Wesleyans, Christian College Coalition members, and other groupings, see Appendices A and B.

3. For a mid-century effort to define "marks" realistically, see D. Elton Trueblood, "The Marks of a Christian College," in VON GRUENINGEN, chap. 11. See also CUNINGGIM C, chap. 1.

4. In 1938–41, CUNINGGIM A; in 1958–61, CUNINGGIM B; in 1978, CUNINGGIM C.

5. See PATTILLO, chap. 12; see also Manning M. Pattillo and Donald M. Mackenzie, *Eight Hundred Colleges Face the Future* (St. Louis: Danforth Foundation, 1965).

6. PATTILLO: quotations—"free because . . . ," 194; "combines . . . ," 195; "colleges purport . . . ," 195.

7. See ANDERSON, 6-7.

8. ANDERSON, *passim*. See also Joe A. Howell and Donald R. Eidson, *The Idea of an Ideal Liberal Arts College* (Lanham, MD.: University Press of America, 1985), chap. 6, which lists ten aspects of a "program to establish a lasting and mutually beneficial relationship between the church and its college" (79). This volume summarizes well the expectations of an earlier time.

9. The quotations come from Thomas R. Giddens, associate dean of Rockford College, "Questionnaire on Church-Related Institutions" (MS, June 1977); see CUNINGGIM C, 23-24.

10. For "groups . . . of the like-minded," see p. 38 and n. 18 of chapter 1, above. The juiciest examples of efforts to "construct a formidable check-list" need not be given chapter and verse, for humane reasons. A case in point: less than five years ago, a Ph.D. was granted (by a second-echelon state university that had little knowledge of church-related colleges) to a study "focused on determining the key issues in renewing church-college relations once the college has been affected by the secularization process." Upward of 200 issues were examined by "21 experts"; the results "indicated that 126 issue statements need to be considered in renewing the [church's name]-college relationship." (Quotations from the dissertation "Abstract," MS, in my files.) But, so far as I am aware, the colleges of the related church have not embarked on any massive effort to comply with "the results." At least from the college's standpoint, piling one upon another mark, or qualification, or requirement, of the college-church relationship is a lost cause.

11. RINGENBERG, especially chap. 4; "The Movement Toward Secularization," 114-146; " . . . perhaps 200," 189.

12. Mark A. Noll, "Introduction," in RINGENBERG.

13. RINGENBERG, chap. 4; quotation from 115.

14. RINGENBERG, "Marks of Secularization," 121-127.

15. RINGENBERG, *passim*. His "Epilogue" (215-220) tries to relieve the prevailing negative tone, but he does not change his restrictive interpretation of "Christian" that, he feels, requires the omission of the "liberal Protestant colleges."

3. Denigrating and Confused Secularists

1. See, for example, ASTIN, chap. 2, "History . . ." The authors note that the "invisible" colleges were loyal to their churches, while the "elite" broke away, but they do not define the terms; 13-19, 25-27.

2. See, for example, ANDERSON: in the comment that "the number of institutions claiming religious affiliation declined from 910 to 790 . . ." during a specified time span, he cites a different source for each figure, with different ways of counting (both sources probably being in error).

See also ASTIN: in chap. 2, the authors' references to church-related colleges show their acceptance of outmoded myths and misunderstandings about governance (23).

3. C. F. Thwing, *op. cit.*, and W. R. Harper, *op. cit.*, were perhaps the most reliable observers of the early twentieth century in taking a balanced view of the place of religion in higher education. See CUNINGGIM A, chap. 2, for a summary discussion and useful bibliography (30-31) of the period.

4. See CUNINGGIM A, chaps. 2 and 4 and Appendix 2. For Phi Beta Kappa chapters in church-related colleges in 1940, see *Phi Beta Kappa Handbook, op.cit.*

5. For partial or total omission of church-related colleges, see chap. 1, n. 7, above. The other side of the neglect issue is that some colleges sometimes have been tempted to whine or, conversely, to boast; see CUNINGGIM B, 28-31.

6. See GREELEY, especially chaps. 1, 2, 4, 5, and 9. He says that "there is neither organizational nor ideological unity within Catholic higher education. . . . almost everything, educationally speaking, can be found . . ."; (2).

7. PACE: Clark, Kerr, "Foreword," xii; Pace, 2, with slight change in wording.

8. See PACE, 104-105, and *passim*. His categorizing of colleges, both "mainline" and "evangelical or fundamentalist," is debatable (22-23); and questions as to whether other emphases may be mistaken arise from a careful reading of 31, 33, 34, 35, 44, 102, 106, and 107. See ASTIN for evidence that Astin and Lee were also relying on "marks"; 13-19, 25-27.

9. RIESMAN A, "New Edition" (1965): re Catholics, 33-35; re Protestants, 36-40; quotation, 36.

10. RIESMAN B.

11. RIESMAN B: chap. 8, "Protestants," 312-333; chap. 9, "Catholics," 334-405. Quotation: "pluralism . . . anarchy," 343; section on "Control," 343-356.

12. RIESMAN B: Quotations: "best Catholic colleges . . ," 355; "triumph of lay professionalism . . . ," 375; "remain 'Catholic' . . . ," 399. GREELEY, 110-11, 114, criticizes *The Academic Revolution* for errors and misunderstandings.

13. RIESMAN B: Quotations: "Natural selection . . . ," 322-328; "net result . . . ," 327.

14. RIESMAN B: Quotations: "several hundred . . . ," 327; "academic over clerical . . . ," 327; "unusual level . . . ," 328.

15. RIESMAN B: "Holdouts Face the Future," 328-33; "cannot compete . . . ," 329.

16. RIESMAN B: Quotations: "survival of recognizably Protestant colleges . . . enclaves." 330. See LYNN: He uses the "survival" phrase as part of the title in his chapter in MARSDEN, and other writers have followed suit by citing the passage.

17. See RIESMAN C, 13-20.

18. RIESMAN C, *passim*.

19. RIESMAN C, *passim*.

20. RIESMAN C, 17, 20. This *Change* article is a revision of chap. 5, "The Limits of Student Choice: The Evangelical Colleges," in Riesman's volume *On Higher Education* (San Francisco: Jossey-Bass, 1980), 162-178. The article repeats his earlier opinions, often in the same words. In his "Preface" to the book, he gives examples of his being "prone to trend thinking that turned out to be overstated if not entirely mistaken" (xix)—a gracious concession by a distinguished scholar—but his attitude to church colleges was not one of his examples.

21. CUNINGGIM C (a Section of PARSONAGE), chap. 3, 29-42.

22. CUNINGGIM C, 32-39.

23. CUNINGGIM C, 37-41.

4. Neoconservatives: Wistful and Assertive

1. See PARSONAGE: "Questions for Institutional and Denominational Self-Study," 107-13; chap. 6, "An Overview of Current Denominational Policies and Studies in Higher Education," 189-301. Perhaps the most ambitious program of any church has been that of the "Commission on United Methodist Higher Education," set up by F. Thomas Trotter in 1973 and described in his Foreword, above (00). The makeup of the Commission was somewhat ecumenical, and the "main report" of its six published volumes was *A College-Related Church* (Nashville, 1976), which "redefined the questions about church and college relationships." See also TROTTER, chaps. 11-19.

2. See HUTCHESON, 838-41.

3. HUTCHESON, 839-840.

Notes

4. HUTCHESON, *passim;* quotation, 839.

5. HUTCHESON, 840.

6. *Christian Century*, October 26, 1988, 964, and November 2, 1988, 996-97.

7. F. Thomas Trotter, "The College as the Church's Gift," and Hutcheson's reply, *Christian Century*, November 30, 1988, 1098-1101. See TROTTER, *passim,* for a fuller treatment of his position.

In LYNN, 189-91, there is a helpful discussion of the Hutcheson-Trotter "exchange of views." On only one point would I enter a demurrer: Lynn feels that Hutcheson's view "bears a striking resemblance to Howard Lowry's portrait forty years earlier"; but it seems to me that Lowry would have much more in common with Trotter. See Howard Lowry, *The Mind's Adventure* (Philadelphia: Westminster Press, 1950).

8. Arthur J. De Jong, *Reclaiming a Mission: New Directions for the Church-Related College* (Grand Rapids: Eerdmans, 1990). Reviews were by Michael A. Maus: in *Christian Century*, February 6-13, 1991, 171-73, and *AGB Reports*, May-June 1991, 32-34.

9. For scholars who believe that the church-related college has declined along with the mainline church, see BASS A and B; John M. Mulder, "Presbyterians and Higher Education: The Demise of a Tradition?" (MS, Association of Presbyterian Colleges and Universities, March 1990).

10. See, for example, John F. Crosby, "Education and the Mind Redeemed," *First Things*, December 1991, 23-28; and HAUERWAS, MARSDEN, and BURTCHAELL, as referred to in succeeding paragraphs.

11. See George M. Marsden, "Is There a Place for Christianity at Duke?" *Duke Dialogue*, March 13, 1992; David W. Lutz, "Can Notre Dame Be Saved?" *First Things*, January 1992.

12. HAUERWAS, 221, 222.

13. HAUERWAS, 223-34. Quotations are from 223; "[D]o we have a church . . . ?" is printed in italics.

14. HAUERWAS, 237, 238. This essay was also printed in *Katallagete* 9, Summer 1986, with the subtitle, "Church and University in a Confused Age."

15. HAUERWAS, 249, 250. For a recent debate of these and related issues that puts Hauerwas's neoconservative point of view under scrutiny, see *Soundings*, Winter 1992: Beverly A. Asbury (Chaplain at Vanderbilt), "Campus Life in a Time of Culture War," 465-75; Stanley Hauerwas, "A Non-Violent Proposal for Christian Participation in the Culture Wars," 477-92; and Asbury, "A Reply to Hauerwas," 493-97. *Soundings*, Winter 1993, returned to the debate: Julian N. Hartt (Kenan Professor of Religious Studies Emeritus, Univ. of Virginia), "Moral Unintelligibility? A Commentary on the Asbury-Hauerwas Debate," 591-602.

16. CUNINGGIM A, 142-51, 239-40; Michaelsen, *op. cit.*; BASS B, 221-22; Paul Ramsey and John F. Wilson, eds., *The Study of Religion in Colleges and Universities* (Princeton: Princeton Univ. Press, 1970).

17. See Harry E. Smith, *Secularization and the University* (Richmond: John Knox Press, 1968), especially "The Expansion and Revision of the Curriculum," 102-14.

18. In MARSDEN, chap. 1, "The Soul of the American University: An Historical Overview," is Marsden's alone, 9-45.

19. MARSDEN, 9; 41 n. 3. See my discussion of Hutcheson's point of view, pp. (66-67), above.

20. MARSDEN, 11-12.

21. MARSDEN, 13-37; " . . . baseball team," 33; "unique perspectives . . . ridiculed," 37.

22. MARSDEN, 37-41: " . . . apply professions . . . more consistently," 38; " . . . building distinctly Christian institutions. . . . ," 41. Marsden's book, *The Soul of the American University: From Protestant Establishment to Established Nonbelief* (New York: Oxford Univ. Press, 1994), was not available when I wrote, but the publisher's description suggests that he has continued in the line of thought here described; see also his op-ed piece, "Church, State and Campus," *New York Times*, April 26, 1994.

23. BURTCHAELL, Part 1, 16-29, and Part 2, 30-38. "The Drift . . . " was an earlier MS version, dated August 15, 1990.

24. BURTCHAELL, Part 1, 17; use of "secularization" in his MS "The Drift . . . ," 2.

25. BURTCHAELL, Part 1, 17, 18. The history to which Burtchaell referred was CONKIN; the story of Vanderbilt's separation from the Methodist Church is largely in chap. 8, "The Bishops' War," 149-184.

26. BURTCHAELL, Part 1, 18-21, and Part 2, 30, 37. Compare with CONKIN, 149-184; and with Edwin Mims, *Chancellor Kirkland of Vanderbilt* (Nashville: Vanderbilt Univ. Press, 1940), and his *History of Vanderbilt University* (Nashville: Vanderbilt Univ. Press, 1946), Part 2.

27. BURTCHAELL, Part 1, 21; CONKIN, 171-184; Mims, *History of Vanderbilt University, op. cit.*, 291-318. Conkin reported that the Church's General Conference vote for "complete" severance was 154 to 131 (184). But a participant, who was also a college president (Wofford), wrote that the key vote was even closer, 150 to 140; see Henry Nelson Snyder, *An Educational Odyssey* (Nashville: Abingdon-Cokesbury, 1947), 190-196.

28. BURTCHAELL, Part 1, 22-29.

29. BURTCHAELL, Part 2, 30-32.

30. BURTCHAELL, Part 2: Catholic campuses, 32-36; fifth "moral," 38.

31. BURTCHAELL, Part 2, 38.

5. Discord and Harmony

1. CUNINGGIM A, 50-51, 64; CUNINGGIM B, 2-3.

2. *Yearbook of American and Canadian Churches* (Nashville: Abingdon Press, yearly editions); 1991 has a partial listing of church-related colleges; 1992 omits such a list. Should the Univ. of Bridgeport be listed in Appendix A as being related to the Rev. Sun Myung Moon's Unification Church? Surely not; but see *New York Times*, February 27, 1993.

3. CUNINGGIM B, 3.

4. See CUNINGGIM C, chap. 2.

5. CUNINGGIM C, 82; 89 n. 4.

6. See TROTTER, 143-48 for his discussion of "five distinct pressures that currently afflict church-related colleges": (1) "the retreat from isomorphism"; (2) "the delicate distance from denominations"; (3) "the need for public policy debate on the role of those schools"; (4) "the problem of uninformed church judicatories"; and (5) "the lack of theological reflection." See also McINNES, 19-22; CONN, *passim;* GREELEY, chap. 7, "Problems of Catholic Higher Education."

7. See William W. Van Alstyne, ed., *Freedom and Tenure in the Academy* (Durham: Duke Univ. Press, 1993). Especially relevant are the two chapters posing the supposed problem for church-related colleges: (1) Michael W. McConnell, "Academic Freedom in Religious Colleges and Universities," 303-24, versus. (2) Judith Jarvis Thomson and Mathew W. Finkin, "Academic Freedom and Church-Related Higher Education: A Reply to Prof. McConnell," 419-29. McConnell argues that religious schools should be given some freedom to be less free because of commitments to the church's standards; Thomson/Finkin say no; all should live up to the same standards. Thus they represent the "clash between institutional claims and individual claims of academic freedom" (xi); churches might be more comfortable with (1), whereas the colleges themselves are increasingly comfortable with (2). It is noticeable, however, that both essays assume that old-line definitions of church-related colleges are still reliable.

For the famous Bassett case at Trinity, NC (now Duke), see Snyder, *An Educational Odyssey*, 187-89; Richard Hofstadter and Walter P. Metzger, *The Development of Academic Freedom in the United States* (New York: Columbia Univ. Press, 1955), 445-451. See also William W. May, "Academic Freedom in Church-related Institutions," *Academe*, July-August 1988, 23-28.

8. See KEETON B, *passim*. The largest smorgasbord for campus life problems is probably the daily press, ably abetted by the *Chronicle of Higher Education*. Few scholarly tomes are written about the things that keep presidents awake.

9. For example, in the 1992 Commencement season several Catholic schools were criticized by assorted Cardinals and other Church leaders for giving honors to distinguished laymen who had not always accepted the Church's directions: e.g., Univ. of Notre Dame, Rosemont, Univ. of San Francisco. See Baltimore *Sun*, May 22, 1992; *Chronicle of Higher Education*, May 20, 1992, A-4.

10. For an understanding of this battleground, see McCOY, and Charles S. McCoy's chapter in MAGILL. My baptism in these deep waters did not become total immersion until we went to Perkins, SMU (see Introduction, above); that story is told in Lewis Howard Grimes, *A History of the Perkins School of Theology* (Dallas: SMU Press, 1993), especially chaps. 8-13. See also two essays of mine: "Integration in Professional Education: The Story of Perkins, SMU," *Annals*, The American Academy of Political and Social Science, March, 1956; *Perkins Led the Way: The Story of Desegregation at Southern Methodist University* (Dallas: SMU, 1994).

11. See CONKIN, chap. 8, 149-84. The discussion in chap. 4, above, is in the section, "The Alleged Villainy at Vanderbilt."

12. For example, see Charles F. Cole, ed., *Something More Than Human: Biographies of Leaders in American Methodist Higher Education* (Nashville: United Methodist Board of Higher Education, 1986): cameo biographies of seventeen Methodist educators, chosen not by the colleges but by church officials. See also CONN, chap. 7.

13. When I talk with church-college people about the list of problems, they always respond strongly at the mention of this item. But when I ask, "May I use your college as an example of how lack of support causes strain?" the reply is likely to be, "Oh, don't do that; it would only make things worse." Support by a non-church source has on occasion weaned a college away from its church; see Hollis, *Philanthropic Foundations and Higher Education*.

14. See, for example, KNIGHT, 108-11, for the story of his supporting, when president of Duke, the University of North Carolina (Chapel Hill) in opposition to loyalty oaths, and thus earning Jesse Helms's wrath. See also Earl J. McGrath et al, *Study of Southern Baptist Colleges and Universities* (Nashville: Southern Baptist Convention, 1977). In recent years the Southern Baptists have perhaps exceeded all other church groups in giving illustration to the struggle for power as a serious problem for colleges and churches to get tangled in—Baylor, Furman, Mercer, Wake Forest and many another college, as well as all of the Southern Baptist seminaries. But Southern Baptists are not alone; it has happened in nearly all churches at sometime or other.

15. See Alice Cobb, *"Yes, Lord, I'll Do It," Scarritt's Century of Service* (Nashville: Scarritt College, 1987); Jesse Lee Cuninggim, *The Family of God*, (Nashville: Parthenon Press, 1948).

16. See Grimes, *A History of the Perkins School of Theology*; Merrimon Cuninggim, *Perkins Led the Way*.

17. Along with cooling continuity and hot dispute is a third form of temperature-testing contact (or lack of it): icy distance. Naming some colleges where "the question of relationship with parent church arose," I did not name a few others where no such question arose, but should have. When the situation is one of icy distance, with no thaw in sight, then the pretense of relationship should be discarded.

For further references to other firsthand contacts I have had with colleges that treasure their church connection, see Appendix C.

18. In KEETON B, the sympathetic Profile of the Quakers' relationship to Earlham "is a little like that of a conservative parent to a progressive child—affection and some pride, bewilderment and even some dismay, with occasional clashes of will" (289).

See also my article in *Annals, op. cit.*

6. The Archetype

1. Being both free and committed, both independent and church-related, was well stated by William F. Quillian, Jr., president of Randolph-Macon Woman's in "The Faith of a College" (MS, Lynchburg, November 6, 1977). See also McINNES; *A College-Related Church*. Ernest L. Boyer, "Reflections on a Church-Related Higher Education," in *Cresset*, June 1994, 4-8.

2. The Christian College Coalition is a case in point: Appendix A notes several colleges related to one or another denomination who are members, concurrently, of the CCC, a more aggressive "Christian" stance than most denominations take with their institutions. (Appendix B also lists the CCC members who are not related to any church.)

3. See, for example, *Achieving the Mission of Church-Related Institutions of Liberal Learning* (Washington, D.C.: Association of American Colleges, 1977), which reports on a meeting of twenty-seven colleges representing fourteen denominations, held at Rockhurst, November 1976; three colleges for special analysis were Ottawa, Rockhurst, and St. Olaf.

See also PARSONAGE, chap. 6; MAGILL; F. Thomas Trotter, "What Does the Church Expect of Its Colleges?" *Trustee*, June 1979; GODDARD.

4. See SMYLIE; Tewksbury, *Founding of American Colleges*; RINGENBERG.

5. See, for example, F. Champion Ward, "Requiem for the Hutchins College," chap. 2 in John J. MacAleem, ed., *General Education in the Social Sciences*, (Chicago: Univ. of Chicago Press, 1992); William C. DeVane, "A Time and a Place for Liberal Education," *Liberal Education*, May 1964; Henry M. Wriston, *The Nature of a Liberal College* (Appleton: Lawrence Coll. Press, 1937); Lowry, *The Mind's Adventure;* BOYER; KEETON B, especially chap. 5 by Keeton, "The Meaning of a College Education," 259-77; and KEETON A.

6. See Commission on the Humanities, *The Humanities in American Life* (Berkeley: Univ. of California Press, 1980); especially chap. 3, "The Humanities and Higher Education," 60-108.

7. For example, see T. R. McConnell, chairman, Commission to Study Non-Public Higher Education in Illinois, *Strengthening Private Higher Education in Illinois: A Report on the State's Role* (Springfield, IL, 1969). Among the criteria recommended by the Commission for eligibility of colleges to participate in the new program was "that the governing board of the institution possess its own sovereignty . . . [consisting of] final authority in all matters including educational policy, choice of personnel, determination of program and financial management" (63).

8. See LYNN, *passim.;* PARSONAGE: throughout the Parsonage volume, "church-related" is carefully examined.

9. For example, college catalogues have often been a laughingstock, but these days they usually don't deserve to be. Having once studied them at voluminous length (see CUNINGGIM A, Appendices 2 & 3), I can testify to their improvement in recent days, especially in saying a concise and appreciative word about their origins and present character.

10. See Ramsey and Wilson, *The Study of Religion in Colleges and Universities;* MAGILL; PARSONAGE.

11. See LONG; McINNES; SCHWEHN; and of course the great men, John Henry Newman and Alfred North Whitehead.

12. For Derek Bok: *Higher Learning* (Cambridge: Harvard Univ. Press, 1986); and *Universities and the Future of America* (Durham: Duke Univ. Press, 1990).

For Wayne Booth: *The Company We Keep* (Berkeley: Univ. of Calif. Press, 1986); and "The Idea of a University as Seen By a Rhetorician," *Univ. of Chicago Record*, 23, October 13, 1988.

For Ernest L. Boyer, see BOYER.

For Samuel Dubois Cook: "The Meaning and Implications of Church-College Relationships, From the College Perspective: Responsibilities and Expectations" (MS, Address at the Council for Higher Education of the United Church of Christ, May 1, 1980).

For Alice Gallin, OSU: "American Pluralism and Catholic Identity," *Current Issues in Catholic Higher Education*, Winter 1988; and other writings in other numbers of *Current Issues*.

For Morris Keeton, see KEETON A and KEETON B.

For Nannerl Keohane: "The Mission of the Research University," *Daedalus*, Fall 1993; and her inaugural address as President of Duke Univ. (MS, Durham, October 23, 1993).

For Douglas M. Knight, see KNIGHT.

For James T. Laney: "The Education of the Heart," *Harvard Magazine*, September-October 1985.

For Edward LeRoy Long, Jr., see LONG; and "Religion and Ethics in Value-oriented Higher Education," *Society for Values in Higher Education Newsletter*, April 1944.

For Charles S. McCoy, see McCOY; and "The Church-Related College in American Society," in MAGILL.

For Neal Malicky: "Time Capsules, Space Capsules and More," *Presidential Papers* (Nashville: United Methodist Board of Higher Education, November 1991).

For Benjamin E. Mays: *Born to Rebel* (New York: Scribners, 1971); and *The Relevance of Mordecai Wyatt Johnson for Our Times* (Washingdon, D.C.: Howard Univ., 1978).

For Richard Morrill, see MORRILL.

For William F. Quillian, Jr.: "The Faith of a College"; and "Apologia pro Vita Mea," *Alumnae Bulletin,* Randolph-Macon Woman's College, Lynchburg, November 1952.

For Paul C. Reinert, SJ, see REINERT.

For Harry E. Smith: *Secularization and the University;* and "Theological Principles Which Shape Presbyterian-Related Colleges," *Presbyterian Outlook*, October 1993.

For F. Thomas Trotter, see TROTTER and other books cited in these notes.

For Richard Wood: Opening convocation addresses at Earlham, Richmond, IN: 1985, "Improbable Society—Improvable Society"; 1986, "A Sturdy Appreciation of Society"; and 1990, "Because Earlham is a Quaker College . . . "

13. See Jaroslav Pelikan, *The Idea of the University: A Reexamination* (New Haven: Yale Univ. Press, 1992): Pelikan shows that Newman still speaks to the academy, and many of his ideas are relevant today. But ultraconservatives find little to please them in today's college; see Allan Bloom, *The Closing of the American Mind* (New York: Simon & Schuster, 1987), and Dinesh D'Souza, *Illiberal Education* (New York: Free Press, 1991).

14. DYKSTRA, 63, 65; and his *Vision and Character* (New York: Paulist Press, 1981), especially the section "Character and Community," 55-58. See also Myron B. Bloy, Jr., "Faith Communities in the Academic World," in CROSSCURRENTS, 437-52; and LONG, especially chap. 4, "The Significance of Community for the Institution of Learning," 45-56.

15. SCHWEHN, 41, 45, 61-62.

16. SCHWEHN, 135, 136.

17. SCHWEHN, 80-81.

18. SCHWEHN, 94. See also his "The Once and Future University," in CROSSCUR-RENTS, 453-462, in which he discusses "three related challenges to the present-day academy: its need to recover and clarify a proper sense of purpose; its need to refurbish the ideal of objectivity; and its need to insure that multiculturalism is creative and constructive rather than destructive" (454).

19. See, for example, DYKSTRA, 62 ("values are thin reeds . . . "); and SMITH: "There is no term used with more frequency and with greater ambiguity than the term 'value'"(3); but he uses it anyway.

See also Wesley A. Hotchkiss, "Neo-Monachism: A Coming Role for Church-Related Higher Education," 90-98, in MAGILL: " . . . to place values and valuing at the center of the educational process should be the distinguishing character of the church-related college." (96)

20. One of "my" schools, Duke, has been charged with being a hotbed for PC, pro and con; but *Campus*, a national right-wing "student" publication attacking the academy in

general, aimed its Spring 1993 issue maliciously at Duke and its new President before her arrival.

21. For much of SMU's nitty-gritty, see "Report of the University Committee on Intercollegiate Athletics," (MS, SMU, Dallas, May 14, 1987), and "The Bishops' Committee Report on SMU," June 19, 1987. As an AGB consultant at SMU during 1987, I had a chance to witness the positive side of the ordeal; see my "Reform at Southern Methodist University: The Implications for Higher Education," *The American Oxonian*, Spring 1989.

22. See TROTTER; McCOY; CONN, especially chap. 10, sections on "The Question of Spirit" (157-64), "The Question of Essence" (164-71), and "The Question of Common Humanity" (171-173). See also *Current Issues in Catholic Higher Education*; Harry E. Smith, "What's in a Relationship?" *The News of the Presbyterian Church (USA)*, Synod of the Sun edition, November 1993; *A College-Related Church*; Wesley Hotchkiss, *A Unique Role in a Unique Time*, Council for Higher Education, United Church of Christ (no date), and "The College-Church-State Triangle" (MS, March 1980); James I. Spainhower, "Church-Related Higher Education for the 21st Century" (MS, Division of Higher Education, Christian Church [Disciples of Christ], March 1990), and "In Pursuit of the Best" ibid. (MS, October 1991).

7. Prognosis

1. See Philip E. Jacob, *Changing Values in College* (New Haven: Hazen Foundation, 1957): "Introduction" by Paul Braisted; chap. 6, 99-116; and SMITH. Quotations: " . . . little or no effect . . . ," from Jacob, 58; "basic values . . . largely constant . . . ," from SMITH, 8.

See also: Edward D. Eddy, *The College Influence on Student Character* (Washington, D.C.: American Council on Education, 1959); W. Max Wise, *They Come for the Best of Reasons*, ACE, 1958. For a recent study showing that "college learning can have important moral consequences," see James R. Best, "Research on Moral Judgment in College Students," in Garrod and Andrew, eds., *Approaches to Moral Development* (New York: Teachers Coll. Press, 1993). (I am indebted to Edward L. Long, Jr., for this citation from his "Religion and Ethics in Value-Oriented Higher Education," op.cit.)

2. See MORRILL: Edward D. Eddy, "Foreword," xi-xii.

3. See PACE, chaps. 4 and 5. For Quaker colleges, see (Haverford) Douglas H. Heath, *Fulfilling Lives: Paths to Maturity and Success* (San Francisco: Jossey-Bass, 1991); (Guilford) Elizabeth B. Keiser and R. Melvin Keiser, "Quaker Principles in the Crucible of Practice," CROSSCURRENTS, 476-84. For Wheaton: see KEETON B, "Wheaton College (Illinois)," 17-45; and Michael S. Hamilton, "Fundamentalism and Education at Wheaton College," CROSSCURRENTS, 469-76. Also in CROSSCURRENTS: Marvin Fox, "Jewishness and Judaism at Brandeis University," 464-69.

4. See CONN, "Foreword," and 164-65. The collegiate world has been more ecumenical than the churches since the heyday of the Student Christian Movement (SCM), the Intercollegiate YMCA and YWCA, and the Student Volunteer Movement. Nothing has quite taken the place of the old SCM, and its spirit in various modern guises is still around the campus. As some churches seem to have declined in their enthusiasm for ecumenicity, or never to have had it, perhaps the colleges will newly discover its benefits.

Appendix C: Church-related Colleges and Values

1. See *Annual Reports* of the Edward W. Hazen Foundation, New Haven, and the Danforth Foundation, St. Louis, in the 1950s and 1960s; *The Danforth Associate Directory*, St. Louis, 1978–79, 1979–80.

2. See PARSONAGE, chap. 3.

3. See periodic *Reports*, Board-Mentor Program, Association of Governing Boards of Colleges and Universities, Washington, D.C.

4. See [Ken Yamada, ed.], *1994 Directory* [of Colleges, Universities and Theological Schools], United Methodist Church; cf. listing of UMC institutions in Appendix B.

5. See *network Communique*, Newsletter of the Lilly Fellows Program in Humanities and the Arts, Valparaiso Univ., vol. 2, Fall 1993, *Cresset,* June 1994.

6. See *Phi Beta Kappa, A Handbook for New Members, 1991–1994*, 22-28.

Index

Index

Butts, R. Freeman, 181

California Lutheran Univ., 175
California, Univ. of, Berkeley, 119
Carleton Coll., 176
Carnegie Commission on Higher Education, 36, 55, 56
Carnegie Corporation, 26
Carnegie Foundation for the Advancement of Teaching, 34
Carroll Coll. (MT), 177
Carroll Coll. (WI), 177
Catawba Coll., 90, 174
Catholic Univ., 29, 176
Catholics. *See* Roman Catholics
Centenary Coll. (LA), 174
Central Methodist Coll., 174
Centre Coll. (KY), 122, 176
Change Magazine, 180, 185
Chicago, Univ. of, 18, 26, 29, 119
Christian and Missionary Alliance, 152
Christian Century, 66-67, 179, 186
Christian College Coalition, 38, 42, 67, 119, 123, 171-72, 183, 189
Chronicle of Higher Education, 32, 183, 188
Church of God, 70, 153
Church of the Nazarene, 154
Church of the New Jerusalem, 80, 154
Church of Christ, 49, 59, 60, 152
Clark Univ., 26
Clark Atlanta Univ., 90, 174
Clebsch, William, 14
Cobb, Alice, 189
Coe Coll., 176
Cole, Charles F., 188
Columbia Univ., 25, 47
Concordia Coll. (NE), 174, 175
Concordia Coll. (Moorhead) (MN), 175
Conkin, Paul K., 73, 74, 178, 187, 188
Conn, Robert H., 178, 183, 188, 192
Cook, Samuel Dubois, 103, 190
Cornell Coll. (IA), 174, 176
Cornell Univ., 26
Covenant College, 183

Cox, Harvey, 182
Creighton Univ., 175
Crosby, John F., 186
Crosscurrents, 178, 191, 192
Culver-Stockton Coll., 177
Cumberland Univ. (TN), 90, 174
Cuninggim, Jesse Lee, 89, 189
Cuninggim, Merrimon, 178 et seg.
Curran, Charles E., 182
Current Issues in Catholic Higher Education, 182, 190, 192

Dakota Wesleyan Univ., 174
Dallas, Univ. of, 29, 55, 176
Danforth Foundation, 17-18, 90, 173, 193
Dartmouth Coll., 25, 28
David Lipscomb Univ., 177
Davidson Coll., 29, 59, 175, 176
Davis and Elkins Coll., 66
Dayton, Univ. of, 29
De Jong, Arthur J., 67, 186
Denison Univ., 17, 89
Denver, Univ. of, 29, 90, 174, 176
De Paul Univ., 177
DePauw Univ., 174, 176
Detroit, Univ. of, 29
DeVane, William C., 190
Dickinson Coll., 174, 176
Dillard Univ., 174
Dillenberger, John, 182
Dirks, J. Edward, 182
Disciples (Christian Church), 37, 66, 80, 154, 192
Doane Coll., 177
Drake Univ., 176
Drew Univ., 175, 176
Drury Coll., 174
D'Souza, Dinesh, 104, 191
Duke Univ., 17, 30, 42, 68, 69, 75, 175, 176, 188, 192
Dykstra, Craig, 104, 106, 178, 191

Earlham Coll, 176, 189, 191
Eastern Mennonite Coll., 29
Eckerd Coll., 30, 177

196

Index